Grave's End

The pressure on my chest radiates to my shoulders, pressing them into the bed. It's as if a liquid weight has spread itself all over my body, paralyzing my limbs and torso, allowing me to breathe, but denying me the ability to move.

I struggle to open my eyes, but achieve nothing but frustration and failure. I am not asleep. I am fully conscious, in a state of panic unthinkable during the day, intolerable in the dark of night, held prisoner by some tortured, invisible presence, insistent on abruptly invading my slumber. The more I struggle toward freedom, the more I am pushed into the mattress, perspiring, heart palpitating, a scream involuntarily silenced within my throat. Some nights I experience my skin being stroked while I fight to regain control of my body, my sight. Thank God, this was not one of those nights. Tonight it lets me open my eyes, shaken but unviolated, frightened, but not as frightened as I know I can become.

About the Author

Elaine Mercado is a registered nurse from Brooklyn. In addition she is a certified clinical hypnotherapist and a certified CPR instructor. As an ER nurse she became interested in the psychological aspects of patient care, leading her to study and then write about wholistic nursing, focusing on the mind/body/spirit connection, hypnotherapy, visualization, and stress-related disorders. With her second husband, she operates a business called Learning for Life, where they conduct classes teaching CPR to hospital personnel, hotel employees, etc.

To Write to the Author

If you wish to contact the author or would like more information about this book, please write to the author in care of Llewellyn Worldwide and we will forward your request. Both the author and publisher appreciate hearing from you and learning of your enjoyment of this book and how it has helped you. Llewellyn Worldwide cannot guarantee that every letter written to the author can be answered, but all will be forwarded. Please write to:

Elaine Mercado
℅ Llewellyn Worldwide
2143 Wooddale Drive, Dept. 0-7387-0003-7
Woodbury, MN 55125-2989, U.S.A.

Please enclose a self-addressed stamped envelope for reply, or $1.00 to cover costs.
If outside U.S.A., enclose international postal reply coupon.

Many of Llewellyn's authors have websites with additional information and resources. For more information, please visit our website at www.llewellyn.com.

Grave's End
A True Ghost Story

ELAINE MERCADO, R.N.

Llewellyn Publications
Woodbury, Minnesota

First Edition
Eighth Printing, 2006

Book design and editing by Connie Hill
Cover design by Lisa Novak
Cover photo © Mel Curtis / Photonica
Back cover photo of author by Joe Bevilacqua

Library of Congress Cataloging-in-Publication Data
Mercado, Elaine
    Grave's end : a true ghost story/ Elaine Mercado
        p.   cm.

    ISBN 13: 978-0-7387-0003-8
    ISBN 10: 0-73870-003-7 (pbk)

Llewellyn Publications
A Division of Llewellyn Worldwide, Ltd.
2143 Wooddale Drive, Dept. 0-7387-0003-7
Woodbury, MN 55125-2989, U.S.A.
www.llewellyn.com
Llewellyn is a registered trademark of Llewellyn Worldwide, Ltd.

 Printed in the United States of America on recycled paper

Lovingly dedicated to my daughters, Karin and Christine. I thank them for their courage, love, and unending belief in me. I am so proud to be their mother. To my brother, Joe, for his unconditional, unwavering support. To my husband, Matthew, for his patience, love, and contagious spirituality. And to Mom and Dad, for their loving example of what a marriage can be.

Acknowledgement

I would like to thank my brother, Joe Bevilacqua, for pushing, poking, and prodding me to write this book. Were it not for his confidence in me, his love and emotional support throughout my life, there is much I would not have accomplished. Further thanks is due him for his suggestions and expertise in preparing this manuscript.

Introduction

Grave's End by Elaine Mercado is the sort of powerful testimony of a truly observant witness to extraordinary occurrences that makes for impressive reading, especially when one considers that the writer is a trained nurse with a scientific mind-bent.

Having been part of the case at a certain point when my intervention was sought, I can assure the reader that this is exactly how it was. Although parallel cases do occur, the details in this situation were unique and I was able, with the help of medium Marisa Anderson, to alleviate the distressing problem occurring in Mrs. Mercado's home.

But, apart from the factual observations by the author, and her clinical approach in presenting them as the true story it is, the author has a powerful gift with words which makes this story come to life even stronger and better.

Prof. Dr. Hans Holzer

Parapsychologist and Author

Prologue

The story you are about to read is true, to the best of my recollection and the recollections of my family and friends and others involved. It took me a long time to decide to write this book. It took me a long time to accept the fact that my family was living in an apparently "haunted house" . . . and it took me a long time to not feel ashamed about what happened to us.

You may find the contents interesting, absurd, or suspect that the incidents were made up. I would consider this a healthy dose of objectivity. I would react the same way. All I can say to you, again, is that the story is true.

In the early fall of 1982 my husband and I were on our way to look at what was apparently the last affordable house in Brooklyn, New York. We'd been house-hunting for over a year and were very anxious to settle into a home of our own.

At this point in time we were still living in a three-room apartment with our two daughters. Our landlord was extremely frugal with the heat, and we were growing tired of huddling in our living room near a portable heater. We were willing to look at virtually any house within our price range, but we had only a small sum of money available for a down payment. Real-estate agents took us from house to house, showing us lovely homes that, unfortunately, required substantial deposits.

We thought we were permanently stymied until we noticed this one house on their listing. It had been there for over two years, but no one had attempted to show it to us.

"It's too old and too much trouble," one of the brokers said, barely looking up at us, "although you might actually be able to afford this one." The sarcasm in her voice was duly noted. However, we were undaunted by her negative description of the house. We wanted to see it.

So, there we were, full of anticipation, parking our car on this very ordinary block. I was in a very "up" mood that day, partly because I had hopes this would be "the" house, partly because it was fall. September and October had always been my favorite months. The smell of cool air and the vision of trees painted in glowing hues of orange and red and yellow signaled the upcoming holiday season. This particular block had many trees, all colored so vibrantly that the whole area had a beautiful orange cast to it. Newly fallen leaves were gathered in bunches near most of the houses and they crunched beneath our feet as we walked to our latest prospect. I thought of pumpkin pie and chestnuts, and my heart leapt at the thought that perhaps, at last, we had found a house we could actually purchase. Maybe we could even spend Christmas there. I had to stop myself from skipping toward our destination.

As we were walking down the street, I noticed an unusual tree. Not only were its leaves a strikingly colored mixture of orange and red, but it appeared to be almost caressing the house in front of which it was planted. Its trunk was tilted toward the house, with almost no branches extending toward the street. Its branches and foliage sprung out like long arms, almost protectively. When we realized this was the tree in front of the house we were to look at, I felt an unusual sense of peace. I was, without obvious reason, very glad this wonderful, strong tree would be part of the package. I didn't know then that this house, indeed, needed whatever protection it could get.

The house itself was one of those big, old, fat houses; the kind they simply don't build anymore. It was whitish-gray with dark green trim, and rather dingy looking.

In retrospect I could imagine someone describing it as "spooky" looking, but "spooky" was the last thing on our minds. The front yard, not very large, was unkempt. Weeds were growing along the chainlink fence that surrounded it. The four entrance steps were made out of weather-beaten, cracked cement. The wrought-iron railing attached to these steps was rusted and peeling. The front windows, many small ones separated by strips of rotting wood, were nearly opaque with dirt.

For a brief moment, my husband and I looked at each other, wondering if this was such a good idea after all, but we knew our financial situation, and neither one of us wanted to spend another winter with our not-so-friendly landlord. So we took a deep breath and rang the doorbell, half expecting it not to work. To our surprise, we were greeted by a rather pleasant, if somewhat cool, middle-aged couple. They smiled as they brought us up to the second floor of this grand old house.

As we walked up the stairs we were wondering what would be the problem this time. We'd seen so many houses that we developed a knee-jerk reaction of not getting our hopes up. It was hard not to think that, even if the price was right, there would be something terribly wrong. Perhaps there were combative neighbors, or mud in the cellar, or exposed sewer pipes in the kitchen. We'd seen it all by this time. To our surprise, this couple mentioned only one dominant problem—the elderly couple living downstairs. They refused to leave.

"My uncle is one tough cookie," remarked the middle-aged man, his nephew, about the old gentleman inhabiting the first floor apartment. As he reached the top of the stairs, he continued, "My uncle and aunt have been living in this house for over forty years. They sold it to us a few years back and have been paying a nominal rent ever since. I guess he thought this arrangement would go on forever, but our children are grown now and my wife and I bought a house in Florida. We are anxious to leave but my uncle keeps scaring prospective buyers off by declining to move."

My husband and I certainly didn't like the sound of that.

In a few short moments, we found ourselves on the second floor, in the front living room, with windows overlooking the aforementioned beautiful tree. The decor was very bland, no pictures on the walls, no outstanding furniture. It looked like a 1950s motel room. Working our way toward the back of the house, we were introduced to the bathroom, which appeared relatively new. Green and white tiles gleamed at us, reflecting the light on the ceiling. Towels hung on the towel racks, but no pictures or designs of any sort adorned the walls. The shower curtains were, again, green and white, but with no distinguishing pattern. The bathroom was very clean, almost sanitary, but decorated with no imagination, no feeling.

Next to the bathroom was a dining area, connected to a kitchen. Dark wood cabinets dominated this room, and pink, painted-over paneling covered the walls. It wasn't a salmon pink or a "hot" pink, just a dull, almost beige pink, going from ceiling to floor. I could see the texture of the paneling showing through the paint and I wondered why anyone would impose such a nauseating color over wood. I figured I would never find curtains to match this unfortunate hue, but before I could get too upset about the dining room and kitchen, our hosts ushered us into what they termed "the playroom." There, in the back of the house, was a beautiful, spacious area, lined with double windows. It was huge.

"This was built only twenty years ago," the woman said, "and our children spent many hours happily at play here."

I must admit, it was bright and airy and pleasant. A sloped ceiling, punctuated with halogen lights, captured our interest. We imagined our own children playing under this wondrous roof.

Our excitement was palpable. That back room really piqued our interest. Our hosts then brought us up to the third floor and showed us their bedroom, located in the front of the house. It was the largest of the three rooms on that floor, but still it had a sort of restrictive quality to it. Thick, upholstery-like curtains hung on the front windows, almost completely obliterating the radiant sunshine coming through. The spread covering the queen-size bed was heavily quilted and shiny, and reminded me of unwanted afternoons spent at my grandmother's house. I could almost smell the mothballs.

The other two rooms were nearly claustrophobic in nature—bedrooms housing the remnant memories of their now-moved-away children. The walls were devoid of decoration, except for a Charles Atlas photo cellophane-taped to one wall. Although there were still beds in each room, no pictures or shelves or toy chests were visible. No posters or telephones or any specific reminders were present. It was impossible to tell if a male or female child had occupied either of these rooms. And we didn't ask.

The rooms felt cold and dank. We kept focusing on that airy playroom on the second floor and assumed we could turn even this stark landscape into a warm habitat.

Although the atmosphere upstairs was less than desirable, it was certainly not enough to discourage us. We were finished with our tour when the wife said, "I'm sorry about my husband's aunt and uncle . . . you'd think they'd know better at their age."

"How bad can they be?" I remarked, not quite ready for her response.

"How bad? I'll tell you how bad. They intimidate everyone who comes to see this house. Especially his uncle. He's more than a 'tough cookie'—he's nasty and impossible, and I'm getting sick and tired of it. I don't want to live in New York anymore." I could see her husband flinch at her candidness. She continued, "We've got this beautiful house in Florida that we can't move into, and he doesn't give a shit about it. If you can persuade him to move, more power to you. Even the real-estate broker has stopped sending people to see this house. I don't care if this makes us vulnerable to a lower sale price, I want out."

Her husband was clearly not happy with her outburst, but he remained silent, seemingly trying to be tolerant of her obvious frustration.

After a brief, but very pregnant, silence, I exclaimed, "Well, can we meet the ogres downstairs?"

I thought I was being cute, but it wasn't received very well, and I couldn't help but notice my husband's disapproving look. After a moment or two, our hosts took us downstairs, said their goodbyes, and left us alone at the first floor entrance. I suddenly felt frightened. I was anxious about meeting this man and felt my heart palpitate as my husband knocked on the door. I nearly expected Lurch to answer.

My husband looked at me a little strangely and asked if there was anything wrong.

"I'm scared," I said. "Aren't you?"

"Hell, no," he replied. "We can probably get this house for less than we thought."

If it weren't for his attitude, I would have gone home. I straightened my back and waited for the door to open.

We must have knocked three or four times, and I had almost convinced my husband to leave, when the door opened to reveal a short, elderly gentleman. At first glance he looked almost endearing with his yellowish white hair and bowed legs. He was very old, much older than we had expected, perhaps well into his nineties. He was caustic and rude, indicating to us that he was not at all pleased to see yet another prospective buyer.

"We're not leaving, you know," he said with a scowl. "This is our home and no one is ever going to force us out."

It became very clear to us that we were being perceived as the enemy. It was an unfamiliar and very uncomfortable feeling.

"We just want to look at your apartment," my husband said. "We're not at all sure about buying this house anyway."

The old man's expression remained resolute and angry, but he did let us in. He shut the door behind us and we found ourselves in an enclosed porch, one that had once been open. We could still see the original columns vaguely hidden by wood paneling. It was bordered by eight old, green-trimmed, peeling windows. On the floor were ancient tiles and, with a quick glance, I noticed that there was no source of heat in this area. I figured it could only be used in the warmer months.

Leading out of the porch was a beautiful set of French doors made of oak. They had long, narrow panels of beveled glass, reminiscent of late nineteenth-century architecture. They were absolutely gorgeous. We walked through these doors to a small narrow foyer, with the living room on the right. We were very disappointed.

This room was very small, perhaps ten by twelve feet, including the bay windows facing the enclosed porch. At an earlier time, these windows had obviously been on the outside wall of the house. There was only room for a full-size couch, perhaps a love seat, and a television. However, at the entrance to this living room, off the foyer, we noticed doors that were inserted into the walls. We had never seen this before, except in old movies. We were instantly charmed. The house must have been more than a hundred years old. Even though the old man was grumpy and impatient, we were still charmed. We noticed the doilies covering all of the furniture, and everything seemed to be monotone mahogany. It reeked of "old." We didn't care. We were very interested in this house.

Beyond the living room was the most glorious dining room we had ever seen. It had a tin ceiling and parquet floor, and there were bay windows on the side wall. It was, of course, the center of the house, even though the mahogany furniture was badly in need of repair. It had incredible potential. On the opposite side of the bay windows was what used to be a fireplace. The wall jutted out about three feet deep, five feet wide. My mind began racing with thoughts about reconstructing the original fireplace. I thought of warm family dinners held within the walls of this great room. The doilies were easy to dismiss in this most fetching arrangement. Even the old man's obvious contempt was easy to ignore, until he ushered us into the back rooms.

The experience of the dining room faded soon after we entered the kitchen. It was completely gray. Floors, walls, cabinets—all gray, and in desperate shape. It was a small room with two entrances. The kitchen was on the other side of the dining room, behind a wall, with the fireplace part in the middle. One entrance was at the beginning of the dining room, the other at the far end. A person could literally go around in a circle, past the fireplace, and still end up in the kitchen. Two hip-high windows faced an alley, a small table was in the center and a few gray cabinets hung above a rusted sink. It was depressing, especially with its one fluorescent bulb flickering on and off.

From the doorway of the kitchen we could, unfortunately, see the bathroom. Actually, we could almost smell it. Any number of subway toilets in Manhattan could easily have put this one to shame. The ceiling paint was peeling, the walls were cracked, and a rusted bathtub on "feet" sat angrily in the center of the room. The toilet bowl and the sink appeared to be unusable.

Our hearts sank. This place needed a lot of work, and perhaps a lot of money. My husband and I looked at each other and realized that, maybe, this wasn't our dream house after all. But we weren't ready to give up yet.

As a sly smile crossed his face, I could tell the old man sensed our waning interest.

"C'mon, folks, let me show you the master bedroom," he said, as he nearly pushed us into a cramped back room.

"Master" bedroom indeed. The room was dark, approximately twelve feet by ten feet. The bed was neatly made and rather attractive drapes hung over its two windows. The ancient bedroom set residing here almost overflowed the dimensions of the room.

After a very brief stay here, he pointed us toward the other back bedroom. He said it had been added on about thirty years ago. It, too, was very small, smaller than the other bedroom. It could almost have passed for a large walk-in closet. There, in a twin bed, lay his wife. The room smelled of sickness. It smelled of medicine and ointments and sadness. His wife of I-don't-know-how-many years looked up at us. She didn't say a word. She was a sweet-faced woman with long white hair combed back into a braid. She had moist, puppy-dog eyes. When she looked at me, my heart just melted. I wondered what had happened in her life to make her appear so vulnerable, so sad.

Suddenly, we felt like intruders. The beauty of the dining room, the thrill of owning our own home, the prospect of living here, faded in the distance. Even if we could afford to fix this house up, we needed the whole house empty. How could we ever ask this couple to leave? Her silent sadness had an impact on us that far surpassed her husband's rage. We were paralyzed. We just wanted to go home.

We bade farewell to the angry old man and went home to our two daughters, our cold three-room apartment, and didn't think about this house again. In a month or so, we received a call from our real-estate agent.

She said the owners had reduced the price even further and the old couple had surprisingly agreed to leave "within a reasonable amount of time." Since my husband needed only the second and third floors for his newly formed business, we decided to buy the house and remain, for the time being, in our miserable apartment. We signed the papers, went to the closing, and, in the early winter of 1982, the house was ours. During the entire process of closing the purchase we never saw the elderly couple. We tried to speak to them once or twice, but they wouldn't open their door. According to their nephew, they were actively looking for an apartment and had resigned themselves to moving. I kept thinking about how sad the old woman looked. My husband and I decided that, no matter what, we wouldn't rush them out.

In the early spring of 1983, we moved the business into the upper two floors. However, the elderly gentleman downstairs demonstrated a great deal of belligerence during this time. He cursed and screamed at any noise we made and insisted that my husband not park in our own driveway. He said he needed the space to fix his many bicycles. He wouldn't let us into the basement. In fact, we had never even seen it. We kept thinking it must be hard for him to vacate a home he had enjoyed for so many years, but he made it very difficult to retain a feeling of sympathy. His wife, on the other hand, never said a word. She just peeked out of the porch windows with those big, sad eyes, and any anger her husband stirred up would quickly dissipate. Even though their lease was legally exhausted we found it very hard to press the issue. My husband, who was generally not a very empathetic man, tried hard to be understanding.

Our patience was, however, growing thin. One year into the ownership of this house found us still living in our cold, damp apartment. Only my husband's business was beginning to thrive. Our family was still cramped and cold, and feeling quite stupid for having bought the house in the first place. Financially, we were now making payments on a mortgage, receiving almost no rent from the old couple, and also paying rent on our apartment.

Sometimes, when the weather was nice, I would put my younger daughter in a stroller, hold my older daughter's hand, and walk over to the office so they could see their father for lunch. The house was only about ten blocks from our apartment.

The old man would always be outside, fixing something, usually a bike. I'd offer a "Hello," but it was never answered. He'd just glare at us. I would continue up the stairs, kids in tow, feeling both sorry for, and resentful of him.

More than eighteen months passed before the couple found an apartment. Two more Christmases had been spent in our apartment, and, at this point, we were all a bit weary of this arrangement.

When they finally moved, we all gathered at the front gate to say "Goodbye," and the old man almost smiled. He even put his hand out, and we shook it. "We got a good deal on a beautiful apartment just a few blocks away," he said.

I forgot all about his being so ornery during this entire process. I was glad that he seemed almost happy. However, his wife just walked slowly down the steps, into their car, never saying a word. I found myself crying because I really did feel badly about making them move.

In that instant, I wasn't sure we'd done the right thing. Even though we had waited more than a reasonable amount of time, even though they didn't seem unhappy about the move, it just didn't seem quite right. I hoped they forgave us for being the ones who ended up buying this house. In my heart, I wished them well, and I meant it.

I comforted myself by remembering that we really didn't put any pressure on them. I think it was just that they were *so* old. I thought of my parents, of myself at that age. I hoped we'd been kind enough to them, even under the circumstances. I was reminded of our patience in this matter when the old man handed me the basement keys. More than a year-and-a-half had gone by and, finally, I was going to see the basement!

Their car drove off, followed by the moving van, and I found myself standing outside, just admiring the beautiful tree, twirling the basement keys in my hand. My husband went back to work upstairs and I, with my children, headed for the basement. We were so excited. The excitement was short-lived.

It was a mess. Two huge oil tanks filled the room, and nuts and bolts and nails and screws were strewn all over the place. It was painted *chartreuse*. The walls were made of cinder blocks, the floor was greasy and painted a dark gray. It was certainly not inhabitable at this time. And it was so small. No one had mentioned to us that this house did not have a full basement. Noticing this now made me understand how inexperienced we'd been at buying a home. We'd never even asked. The basement took up not even two-thirds of the length of the house. The other third was never dug out, and we wondered why this was so.

The next few days we concentrated on moving in all of our stuff. We happily bade farewell to our old apartment and settled nicely into our new, but old, home. What I remember being most happy about was the thermostat. I could regulate our heat! We no longer had to shiver under a pile of blankets or huddle with our children near a heater. I was anxious for it to be cold outside just so I could make it all warm for us.

A few of the neighbors introduced themselves to us, and I asked them if they knew why our basement did not encompass the length of the house. I was surprised when they said that our house had been moved, in its entirety, via a trailer, from its original location around the corner. This move had been accomplished in the early 1940s. The movers had only dug out the existing basement and left what was referred to as the "dirt room." This dirt room was located at the back of the house, under the small bedrooms on the first floor. The only entrance into the dirt room was through two nearly hidden doors, four feet from the surface of the floor. Basically, it was a crawl space. We thought it odd at the time, but never seriously questioned it. We just felt disappointed that the basement was so small.

On one of the first few days of our move we invited a number of family members to help us with unpacking our belongings. Among them was my brother, Joe.

When he first entered the basement he got what he later described as a "very unnerving feeling," as though he was being watched. He chose not to share this eerie experience with any of us. He later explained that he figured, since we had already purchased the house, he would not disturb us with what might have been just his imagination. But, on that day, with my whole family around us, everything seemed just fine.

Within two or three days we were all moved in. The kids were snug in their beds in the very small back room, and my husband and I took over the somewhat larger master bedroom. Within a few days, and without knowing what my brother had felt in our basement, I began to be aware of being "watched." I felt like someone was always sort of looking over my shoulder. I'd turn around, half expecting to see one of my children, or my husband, and no one would be there. I attributed this strange feeling to my being overwhelmed with the move and I tried to disregard it. I had always been a die-hard disbeliever in the the supernatural, so the thought of anything odd never entered my mind. I also became quite distracted by the fact that I was finally a home owner. I could control our heat, and I did not have to make any more trips to the laundry. There was a washer and dryer in the basement. My very own washer and dryer.

My children were warm, we had a back yard and a driveway, and I was now permanently relieved of laundromat duty. I felt pretty good about things in general, but there was one thing on my mind that I was hoping the purchase of this house would alleviate. I had been aware for some time that my marriage was not a very good one.

I tried to push this thought out of my mind and concentrate on all the stuff I needed to do to get our house into shape. But, in my quiet moments, my marital woes would catch up with me. It wasn't just our old apartment that caused friction, it was our relationship itself. We'd been arguing since the inception of our marriage, but the last year or two had been terrible. I thought a new environment might bring new hopes of invigorating what was quickly becoming a cold and distant relationship. This thought made me start fixing the house right away. We started with the bathroom. The worse I felt about our marriage, the harder I clung to the fantasy that making things better on the outside might make things better on the inside.

Making the bathroom usable was the only real initial investment we made in the house. We redecorated the walls with flowered blue tiles from Italy and put in a shiny new white floor. We matched the tiles with a powder-blue sink, toilet, and bathtub. I was so proud of how nice it looked. It did not even remotely resemble the antiquated and foul bathroom that had existed only weeks ago. We couldn't afford to modernize any other area, so the fixing-up ended here. I couldn't help but feel like I was waiting to see if a new house, a new bathroom, might change things between me and my husband. It was a silly notion to grasp at, but it seemed a very real possibility to me.

By the time all this was done and we were really settled in, our eldest daughter, Karin, was eleven years old and our youngest, Christine, was five. They were happy (when their parents weren't fighting), although a bit crowded, in that small back bedroom. We installed bunk beds in the hope of helping them out, although we knew that in time, as they grew older, this room would not be big enough for both of them. We figured that by then our financial situation would change and we would be able to afford to finish the nuts-and-bolts basement. One of them, most likely Karin, could move down there into a new bedroom. For the moment, they were reasonably comfortable. Unlike in our old apartment, they were waking up to the warm, cuddly sound of heat bubbling up through the radiators. Whenever I saw them sleeping, it warmed my heart to know they no longer had to wake up freezing in the middle of the night.

It was a very good feeling.

As the days and weeks wore on, the feeling of being watched became more troublesome. It started to produce a sensation at the top of my back, in between my shoulder blades. It wasn't an itch, but rather a tingling feeling. I had to fight the urge to look behind me—and the urge always won. No one else said anything about this, so neither did I. This odd sensation occurred at varying times during the day and night. It was quite unnerving. One night, after being particularly troubled by these feelings, I approached my husband.

"Ever feel anything unusual upstairs in your office?" I asked.

"Not really." he replied. "What do you mean, unusual?"

"Well, like someone is watching over your shoulder, or standing right behind you. Sometimes I feel that way, especially when I'm folding laundry, or cooking dinner. Like someone is with me, but not really."

His admonishment was swift. "You must be imagining things. I've never felt anything like that. What are you talking about anyway? Get a grip."

"Get a grip," indeed. I hated that phrase. It implied losing one's perception of reality. I was so sorry I'd said anything to him. I chastised myself for not knowing better.

He was already very unhappy with me, already at the point where criticizing me was becoming a daily event. All I did was give him more fuel for his fire. We were only in the house a few months at this point, and I already could see that nothing between us was going to change. After this brief, dismissive exchange, I went outside and sat down on our front steps (the "stoop," as it is referred to in Brooklyn) and collected my thoughts. I knew I wouldn't mention these uncomfortable feelings to him again. I promised myself I would just ignore them and hope for the best. I also recognized that the more successful his business became, the farther apart we were growing. I didn't know why, but I just knew we were moving in distinctly different directions.

I decided, only a few weeks later, to go to college with the goal of becoming a registered nurse. My husband was sure I wouldn't make it through the first class and treated the whole idea rather condescendingly.

"Sure, honey, you go ahead and take your classes," he would say with a wry smile.

I hated that reaction. I wanted to be taken seriously. It was very disheartening to realize that my husband was treating this as some sort of a whim. I really wanted to become a nurse.

In a short while, after receiving my first "A", nursing school became a very important part of my existence. At first I went only in the evening, staying at home during the day to care for our children. Later on I arranged with my parents to pick up my children at 3 P.M. and I was still able to be there most days for Christine's lunch hour. Karin was in sixth grade and Christine was in first. I felt I was doing a good job covering all my bases, but the longer I stayed in school, the angrier my husband got. I tried to explain to him that becoming a nurse was the fulfillment of a lifelong goal. I had wanted to be in a helping profession ever since I was a child. I think he knew, as well as I did, consciously or subconsciously, that if I completed my education, I would no longer be as financially dependent on him as I was at that time. I was absolutely determined to graduate and go on to practice nursing. He was not in the least thrilled with my resolve.

Between my difficult marriage, raising two children, dealing with the house and attending nursing school, the "watching" feelings became rather unimportant. They were there, but I forced them into the background as much as possible. Several times a day I would be prodded to look over my shoulder at an unseen entity, sure someone would come into focus, sure it was just the kids or the dog. No one was ever there at these times and I made myself think the feelings would go away if I got all the stress out of my life. Feeling like I was being watched had much less power than my preoccupation with my failing marriage. I put those unpleasant sensations out of my mind for quite some time.

We were in the house nearly a year. My children were doing well in school, I had just finished another semester in college and my husband's business was doing very well. Our relationship, however, remained argumentative and distant. Although I was able to deal with the feelings of being watched, a disturbing new sensation arose. I began to feel frightened of being alone in our house. I had never experienced anything like this before. I'd come home from school, knowing I'd have to pick-up my daughters at my parent's house in an hour or two, knowing that my husband was at a meeting in New Jersey or somewhere, and I'd sit down to study. Suddenly, I'd be aware of *not* being alone at all. The house felt occupied somehow.

The feeling would make me shudder and move my shoulders up and down, trying to shake it off.

It wasn't long before I'd covertly try to always have someone at home. I'd get my kids early, or study on those days when I knew my husband was at his desk upstairs. I felt rather foolish doing this, but the feeling was so uncomfortable.

It was around this time that Karin began having some unusual sensations herself. She told me she heard strange noises coming from the inside of our bathroom hamper. She described them as sounding like "clawing" or "scratching" noises. Very distinct. Very clear.

My husband and I figured that a rat, or some other form of rodent, must have gotten into the hamper. We emptied it, took out all the clothes, examined everything. No rat, no mouse. She was insistent.

"I heard it, Mommy, I heard it while I was taking a bath."

We attributed her reaction to an overactive imagination. Unfortunately, we attributed way too much in this regard.

One evening, when Karin was lying on the living room couch, she saw Christine go into their bedroom located in the back of the house. Karin got up and followed her, but when she got to the bedroom, Christine was not there. Karin became bewildered and frightened. She came running to me, sincerely upset.

"Mommy, I saw Chris go into the bedroom, but she's not there. Where is she, where is she?"

I called Chris's name and she answered from the bathroom. She hadn't been in her room all night. I honestly didn't know what to make of this. I comforted Karin and wondered if perhaps she was experiencing some stress due to our unhappy marriage. This was also the first sign I saw that someone else in the house was having something unusual happen to them.

A few days after this incident, Karin was sitting on the bunk bed she shared with her sister and told us she saw Christine standing on the chair beside the bed. They chatted for a while. Nothing unusual. However, a few minutes later Chris came into the room! She hadn't been in the room all night. Karin got really scared, and I became concerned about Karin's "imagination." I should have worried about why the house was always so uncomfortable, but I didn't. I kept feeling responsible for what I thought was Karin's increasing level of stress caused by my bad marriage. I hugged her and comforted her, but I didn't tell her about my own experiences, and I silently worried about the damage our marital relationship was having on our children. I also checked up on how she was doing in school, spoke to her guidance counselor. She was well liked and bright and articulate. There didn't seem to be any problem there—only at home. I blamed myself for not being strong enough to repair a failing marriage. All my psychology courses at school came rearing up their ugly heads—I assumed Karin was having a stress reaction to her parent's bad relationship. Unfortunately, my psych courses left no room for the supernatural. Actually, I left no room for it either.

Although I was still feeling watched and could no longer remain home alone, I did not believe Karin's two bizarre experiences of having seen Christine when she wasn't there. I did not connect the happenings. There was nothing in my limited store of knowledge that could enable me to see farther than the obvious. I didn't understand at the time that I should have simply listened to my otherwise healthy, perceptive child. I was too frightened and narrow-minded to entertain the notion that maybe it wasn't Karin's perceptions that were "off." Maybe the house was "off."

2 By the time Karin was thirteen years old, about two years after we moved into the house, it was clear she needed a room of her own. Our previous attempts at manipulating the back bedroom had failed to fit the growing needs of both of our daughters. The space in the nine-by-ten-foot room could stretch only so far. The only other place for Karin to sleep was in the basement. I procrastinated for months before I got up the courage to face the mess down there.

We had the two huge oil tanks removed and replaced them with a gas heater. This heater was placed in a small area in the back part of the basement and we built a wall around it so it wouldn't show. Then we spent two months mucking out everything. There were barrels full of all sorts of objects—nails, screws, old papers, bicycle parts, chains, and lots of small bits of rubber. Anything metal was rusted and everything else was unusable. While we were mucking, we did have some fun. We found postcards dating back to the 1800s. There were faded pictures, old tobacco boxes, and parts of old newspapers. It was interesting to see advertisements for a variety of products now considered either obsolete or laughable. We found nothing of any monetary value, just the kind of stuff that reminded us of a time now past.

None of the memorabilia, except for a postcard signed "Margaret," was in good shape. Most of it crumbled in our hands, especially the newspapers. The few letters in the batch were illegible—the ink had all but faded away. We decided that if we found cards or letters or photos intact, perhaps wrapped up in some box somewhere, we would deliver them to the elderly couple, assuming they were the most likely owners, but no such box was ever discovered. Just bits and pieces of some-one's memories, along with the bits and pieces of junk.

When the basement was finally cleaned, and a new linoleum floor cemented down over the concrete one, we were ready to build a bedroom. My husband hired a contractor, who turned out to be obnoxious and unskilled, but inexpensive enough for us to afford. He built a wall dividing the already small basement into two areas. One would become Karin's room and the other a small den, with enough space for a few bookshelves, a TV and a lounge chair. The contractor put a hole in the upper wall, enough above ground to house an air conditioner. We had to have this option because in the summer, and even in the spring, it became stiflingly hot. There was absolutely no cross-ventilation. There was only one other small window, located in the den part of the basement. In fact, it was so small and so low to the ground outside that I don't think I ever felt a breeze come through it. The contractor then built a clothes closet on the other side of the dividing wall. Voila! Karin had a new bedroom.

We painted the walls a warm pink and added a few shelves and some nice ceiling lights. Three months after we started, Karin moved all her stuff downstairs. She was elated. And so was Christine! That tiny little room upstairs quickly became strewn with all her stuffed animals and books and clothes. In a very short time we wondered how they had ever shared such a small place to begin with. Karin got busy putting up posters and adding her own personal touches. She became very proud of her oh-so-grown-up room.

The construction of our new bathroom upstairs had been confined to only a small area. This newest remodeling involved a much larger space and took a longer period of time. I noticed that the feeling of being watched increased dramatically while Karin's room was being built. It got so bad that I wouldn't go downstairs alone to do the laundry. The laundry room took up a small corner of what was left of the original basement, adjacent to the dirt room. I felt spooked down there, and I felt embarrassed. I didn't know if I was becoming increasingly neurotic or supersensitive to *something*. I didn't want to talk to my husband about this again, but I did decide to discuss it with Karin. I nonchalantly mentioned to her that I felt uncomfortable in the house, especially in the basement.

Her eyes brightened and she said, "Me too, Mom. Sometimes I feel like someone is with me when no one is there. I thought it was my imagination."

She was obviously relieved, but I became frightened. I would no longer venture alone into the place in which my daughter was now sleeping. I began to wonder if it was such a good idea having Karin's bedroom down there. I asked her if she felt uncomfortable sleeping in her new room.

She replied, "No more than usual."

No more than usual? She refused to elaborate. She also refused to come back upstairs. I wished I'd put a folding bed in the living room instead of building her a new room in this basement of ours.

I told my husband about our conversation, but he said I had put ideas into her head. We talked that night over dinner, with the children there, about the feelings of being watched. To my surprise, Christine echoed Karin and myself. She was only seven years old at the time, but she was pretty articulate. She said she felt like looking over her shoulder when she was upstairs in the dining room. Then she happily went on eating her meal. My husband thought we were all crazy. I began to worry—a lot.

It wasn't long before a bevy of Karin's friends started visiting her new room. It also wasn't long before they started investigating other parts of the basement, most notably that dirt room. None of us had ever opened the entrance doors. The crawl space was only about two feet high and the doors were at least four feet above the basement floor. In order to get in there a person would have to stand on a chair, open the doors, and lift themselves into it. I think for teenagers this seemed like an open invitation for exploration.

I didn't know Karin and her friends had been exploring this area. I did know that the unnerving feelings had been on the increase. This increase took the form of escalating sensations that resembled what a person might feel when they are being examined without their knowledge—as if someone, or something, was behind an invisible plate-glass window, staring at me intensely. It happened in the kitchen when I was cooking dinner, or on the telephone. It happened in the dining room, the living room, and my bedroom, even in the bathroom. The feeling usually passed within a few minutes, but sometimes it would linger and I'd go from room to room, all the while feeling ridiculous. But nowhere in the house did it happen more often than in the basement. There, at the laundry area, I found it impossible to shake or ignore the sensations.

I also started hearing footsteps going down the basement stairs at times when I couldn't arrange for anyone else to be at home with me. The steps sounded heavy and purposeful. At these times when I had to be alone, I found myself staying in one room, immersing myself in nursing books, trying to ignore the unnerving sensations surrounding me. They didn't happen every day, they didn't happen every time I was alone in the house. They just happened often enough to make me nervous and jittery, just enough to throw me off guard. I certainly didn't connect the increase of these feelings in any way with the explorations of the dirt room.

The girls were going in and out of this space on a regular basis. One day they came upstairs, all excited, holding an ancient lantern. It was made of red glass and rusted metal. It brought scenes to mind of the horse and buggy era. I could just imagine it being swung by a footman, warning a horse to stop. I took the lantern and went downstairs with them. The doors to the crawl space were wide open and the smell coming from this room was very unattractive—not mildew, not stale, but rather foul. I closed the doors and told them to stop going in there. I thought it was unsafe and unclean. I had no idea at the time what *else* this room represented. I couldn't bear to go anywhere near it and I couldn't understand how they actually crawled inside of it. The negative effect of opening these doors would be with us for years to come.

Although Karin seemed happy to be occupying her new room, her behavior changed. She seemed almost remote somehow. She had always been a very private person, even as a very young child. She was never one to blurt out her feelings, and it was hard for her to cry. She tended to keep things to herself, but this was different.

Her remoteness took the form of locking herself in her room. She had never done that before. Her schoolwork remained the same, and she had the same friends. She didn't seem particularly unhappy. But, early in the evening, she would somberly go downstairs, and lock the door of her room. I knew that budding adolescents treasure their privacy, so in the beginning this didn't bother me. We'd already talked at length about the bad feelings I got in the laundry room and she stated, very succinctly, that those feelings did not bother her. She ignored them and was not frightened at all. But I remained concerned and worried—something was not right.

I was brought up in a strict Pentecostal church, a Bible-toting, talking-in-tongues, rolling-on-the-floor type of church. It scared the hell out of me. By the time I was eighteen, I had decided to remain a Christian, but I would never again belong to any organized religion. It took me easily until my early thirties to do away with most, but not all, of the guilt induced by the teaching of my formative years. It had been a real struggle for me and I was careful not to introduce my children to anything even remotely resembling what I had to go through. I taught them about Christ, about the Bible, but very informally, very matter of fact. I wanted them to know what Christmas and Easter were all about, but I wanted them to make their own decisions concerning what they would eventually believe. I felt that whatever brought them comfort and joy would be okay with me. My husband was a Catholic who had not followed his religion for years. At our dinner table there were discussions about the usual "things of the day," and there were also a lot of lively conversations concerning the mysteries and wonders of life, but virtually no references to organized religion.

Knowing this, I was very surprised when I went downstairs one day, bracing myself to do the laundry, and heard Karin, behind her locked bedroom door, reciting the Rosary. I didn't know she knew about the Rosary. I didn't interrupt her, but I was very curious about this. I questioned her the next day, but she was very vague about her behavior. I didn't have anything in particular against the Rosary, so I just let it go. I thought perhaps one of her Catholic friends had taught it to her, but I still thought it a little peculiar.

She said the Rosary every day for a while. Once I even peeked through the keyhole of her door and saw her, a very serious expression on her face, holding the Rosary beads, sitting crosslegged, yoga style, in the center of her bed. I thought she looked scared. This time I knocked on her door and told her that I'd been peeking.

She was annoyed at me, and said, rather emphatically, "I am not scared. I am just trying to protect myself."

"Protect yourself from what, Karin?" I asked

"From the dreams I'm having. I have been dreaming about a door, and on it was written the words 'I bestow upon you these certain gifts.' In the dream I'm aware that our new cat has been sent to us to protect us from unwanted spirits. Saying the Rosary seems to make me feel less upset about these dreams, so could you please back off?"

"Okay, Karin," I replied. "I just wanted to know if anything was wrong."

I went back upstairs and remember thinking that she was talking nonsense. She was using such strange terminology for a thirteen-year-old. The cat to which she referred was our newly acquired street cat, whom she named "M-ow." The name came from the sound the cat made whenever anyone came close to her. She'd been an outside cat for over a year and hung out near our house day and night. I refused to bring her in, not being a cat lover. But one day I heard that mournful cry of a cat in trouble and I opened our front door to find M-ow being attacked by a larger, male cat. M-ow had just given birth to a dead fetus and this other cat was still trying to mount her. I chased away the male cat and took M-ow in. She was so sad those first few days, and so affectionate. Poor thing. I was sorry I hadn't taken her in before.

It wasn't long before the cat's affectionate nature changed to a very territorial one. She almost immediately claimed various part of the house as her own. She wouldn't let us pet her unless she was in the mood. I quickly remembered why I didn't like cats, but she grew on us and became part of the family in no time at all.

As Karin was relating that part of her dream concerning M-ow, she stated that M-ow came to her as a protector, that she was to protect her from the "red cat." I had no idea who the "red cat" was, and neither did she. All she knew was that she was sure M-ow was sent to her in this regard. I asked her if she thought her dream had any particular significance, but she said she had no idea. I asked her again if she felt scared, but she denied feeling in any way frightened. I asked her if she was dreaming differently since she'd been sleeping downstairs. She said she was having more *interesting* dreams.

"Maybe you should come back upstairs to sleep, Karin," I said in a rather pleading tone. I really wanted her to stop going down the basement.

"Absolutely not, Mom. I have a beautiful room and I like it down here. I don't want to come back upstairs to that 'baby' room. I'll be fine."

I wasn't so sure.

At this point, we were all dealing with the feelings of being watched. Sometimes I would see Karin studying in the living room and Christine playing in the dining room.

Then, suddenly, they would go someplace else in the house. Karin would try her sister's room, Chris would switch to the kitchen. I was doing the same thing. It was as if we were playing some sort of spiritual musical chairs. This happened so often, we were actually getting used to it.

During this period, I began having sleeping problems, experiencing what I termed "suffocating dreams." I would go to sleep, not especially bothered by anything, and I would awaken moments later, paralyzed in my bed. I was aware of the phenomenon called "sleep paralysis," and I had experienced this from time to time in my life. It's a sort of wake/dream state where someone feels momentarily unable to move. It is quite a common experience. It is also referred to as night terrors. This sensation, however, was very different.

I would fully awaken, already in a paralyzed state, frightened beyond all reason. Fully awake, fully conscious. There was no fuzziness in my thinking, no debate about whether or not I was dreaming. I was not dreaming. I would try to move, but to no avail. I couldn't turn. I could barely breathe. I couldn't speak. There was a pressure on my chest—an all-encompassing, revolting pressure—that would eventually spread over my whole body. It would press me into the bed to the point that I could feel, and see, the mattress indenting. I was terrified and confused.

Along with this immobilization would come the feeling that there was a presence in the room with me—someone or something doing this to me. I also had the sense that I was supposed to know something that I, in fact, did not know. I would try to extricate myself from the pressure, struggling as hard as I could, but it was never hard enough.

It would take as long as it would take. I could never seem to have any control over the length of time these suffocating dreams lasted. Sometimes they were very brief, perhaps lasting a few seconds or longer. Other times, minutes that felt like hours would go by.

The worst part of this experience was that sometimes the pressure was accompanied by invisible strokes directed toward my breasts or inner thighs. This would scare me so much that I would feel a scream well up inside my throat, only to be squelched by the paralyzing pressure. All I could do was wait for it to be over. It invariably left me feeling drained, violated, and dazed. Many times I contemplated the thought that I must be losing my mind. I told no one. I didn't know how to explain what was happening.

These suffocating dreams occurred three or four nights a week, and then, for no apparent reason, would disappear for months at a time. Just when I was sure there was something intolerably strange going on I would get relief and start to rationalize these occurrences as nothing more than nightmares. But I knew there was something more to this, I just didn't know what it could be. Whenever I had experienced sleep paralysis before it never had the connotation of such fear, such terror. I would simply, at some point during the night, wake up in a paralyzed state for a few moments and then be okay. There were no sensations of being touched or having difficulty breathing. No feelings of being pushed into my bed. No sensations of horror. No comparison whatsoever to what I was experiencing during one of these episodes.

I tolerated this in silence for quite some time, until about a year later, when I spoke up. I was having breakfast with my family. The night before had been awful. I'd experienced two or three of these episodes in one night and I was drained and exhausted. As I flipped an omelet on the grill, I had to speak.

"You guys are going to think I'm nuts, but I have been having the worst nightmares. I'm getting up two or three times a night because I wake up being pushed into my mattress, practically suffocated. I can't take it. I feel like someone is in the room with me, like I'm being told something that I can't understand. This has been going on for months and I want it stopped. I don't know what to do." I was crying and felt quite stupid and insane.

"Mommy, the same thing happens to me," Karin said. Her eyes were wide open, relief written all over her face. "I can't move, I can't scream. It happens almost every night, but then it stops for a while. But it doesn't really scare me. Why are you crying so much?"

"Why am I crying? Why? It scares the shit out of me and now I know you feel it, too. I don't want you to experience this. I don't want you to have to deal with this. What the hell is going on here? When did it start for you?"

My husband listened to this with a bemused smile on his face. He didn't take us seriously at all. I wanted to wipe that smile right off his face. Christine said nothing like this had ever happened to her, and I was glad for that. But I kept prodding Karin about trying to remember when these nightmares began.

"Last year," she said, "about the time I moved into my new bedroom."

She was right. That was when they started for me, too. That was when those dirt room doors had been opened, that was when I heard footsteps and felt the watching feelings increase. I wondered what the connection could be between those dirt room doors and our sleeping problems.

The last year had been otherwise uneventful in our house. I was progressing nicely in nursing school, the kids were doing well in their respective schools, and my husband's business was booming. We argued at our usual rate, perhaps a bit more, I was still unhappy in our relationship, but this was nothing out of the ordinary for us.

A few days after this conversation, on a bright autumn morning, Karin awakened, screaming. I ran downstairs to find her in bed; her bedspread and sheets had been pulled off her in a very odd way. The bedspread was in a perfect square, on the floor, pulled off without a wrinkle. This was followed by her blanket and her sheet, with the sheet partially pulled off, nearly all the way to the foot end of her bed. She was sitting up in bed, terrified, screaming that she witnessed the blanket as it was being eased off her bed. She was pale. She was scared. She wasn't kidding.

I looked at my sweet, beautiful fourteen-year-old. She had a look of absolute astonishment on her face. We went upstairs together and Karin slowly calmed down. I was completely mystified at this point. I had no idea what was happening, or what this meant. It was the first time the word "haunted" entered my mind. It was also, unfortunately, the first time I started to doubt my daughter. I think doubting Karin's story was much easier than thinking our house was haunted.

We went to the kitchen and Karin had some orange juice. We sat together at the kitchen table and after a while she began to speak.

"Those blankets just came right off, Mommy. I woke up when the last one, the sheet, was being pulled. I watched it, Mom. Someone pulled them off my bed!"

"But, Karin, *who* did this? Did you see anyone? Was anyone in your room?"

"No, but I felt them there. It was awful."

I didn't know how to handle this situation. I wanted to believe her, but to do so meant exploring some other explanation and I had no idea what that explanation might be. I wondered if she was asking for attention because of the increasing tension between my husband and myself. Maybe she thought I was giving too much attention to her little sister. Maybe college was taking up too much of my time.

I didn't accuse her of making this up, I just decided to listen to her more often and try to pick up any other clues that something might be wrong. I insisted that she sleep upstairs. She balked at this, reiterating that she still loved her basement bedroom. I had no idea how she could still want to be down there, and I wouldn't hear of it. I brought her sheets and blankets upstairs and gave her a choice of sleeping with her sister or on the living room couch. She chose the couch.

It wasn't long before I discovered that she would start the evening on the couch, wait for all of us to go to bed, and then go downstairs to her "wonderful" bedroom. When I got upset about this, she got very angry at me.

"You are so overreacting," she screamed. "Whatever happened didn't hurt me, did it? It's over. Forget it. I want my privacy back!"

My husband heard the argument. He knew about the blanket episode, but he thought we were all out of our minds.

"Let her sleep where she wants," he bellowed. "If she's not scared, don't make her that way."

So, Karin once again began sleeping downstairs, and I continued to deal with my strange nights. We all, now including, by his own admission, my skeptical husband, put up with feelings of being watched most of the time, and the house continued to become more and more of a problem.

I spent a lot of time trying to figure things out. I thought perhaps Karin was frightened that her father and I might end up getting a divorce. When she was very young, maybe ten or eleven years old, she told me she wouldn't mind if we got a divorce because she knew she could live with me and Christine and could still see her father sometimes. I thought this was such grown-up thinking for one so small. She then said most of her friends had this arrangement and I suddenly understood how really sad this situation was. I was sorry our arguments had lead her to this conclusion, sorry her young mind and emotions were forced to deal with such heavy issues. I watched her and waited for some signs of emotional turmoil. I saw none. Except for her admitting to having sleeping problems, and for the blanket episode, she seemed happy most of the time.

I watched myself, too. I started to delay my bedtime, and was happy to catch only a few hours of uninterrupted sleep. I had nothing in my background, in my belief system, that would allow me to explain what was going on. I distracted myself as much as I could. I studied hard, I was very attentive to my children; we were always going to the movies or doing homework or just hanging out. We talked often about feeling watched, but almost never about the suffocating dreams. We tried to pretend they weren't happening. On more than one occasion, visitors to our home remarked that they felt uncomfortable when they found themselves alone, like in the bathroom. They said they felt uneasy. One of them even used the word "watched." They made a joke out of it, and none of us ever admitted to feeling the same, but I filed their comments deep within myself.

I thought of every possible explanation. I tried to be logical. I reasoned that a few unusual things had happened, but this did not necessarily mean the house was haunted. Maybe we were being overreactive, especially me. The nights were not *always* terrifying, the house was not *always* uncomfortable. It would be different if these things happened all the time, like in those movies about haunted houses. And the experiences made no sense, no sense at all. The lights were not flickering on and off, we didn't see any ghostly apparitions. No one had actually been hurt.

I decided to just continue on with our lives as if everything was just fine. But "fine" was not the way it was, nor the way it would be, for a very long time.

3 It wasn't long before I began to feel somehow ashamed about what was going on in the house. I was frightened that there might be something wrong with me, something almost humiliating. When I lost a night's sleep to unrelenting suffocating dreams, when I lay awake listening to unseen footsteps until the wee hours of the morning, I wondered if perhaps I was under too much stress. Maybe enduring my difficult marriage, attending nursing school, and taking care of my children might be proving too much for me. I didn't *feel* crazy, but I was concerned. My husband thought this was all nonsense. When I tried to bring up the subject with my parents, they just stared at me in disbelief. Except for my brother, Joe, there was no one I felt could understand, never mind explain, what was happening to us.

Joe listened to me with a great deal of interest. He felt something was wrong with the house, not with me. Although he'd had no experience dealing with this subject, his kind words and compassion, and his open mind, helped me to cope on many occasions.

My children, were, of course, my partners in these experiences. We would even joke about having to move from room to room to avoid being watched, but as the adult, I felt it was my responsibility to offer some reasonable explanations.

I had none. I felt quite frustrated and, worse, unable to provide them with a comfortable feeling at home. I wanted to make everything okay, but I didn't know how.

I had started seeing a therapist a few years before we moved into this house. He helped me deal with the guilt about leaving church, helped me deal with the anxiety, even panic attacks, that had plagued me since childhood. He helped me understand that I was a capable, intelligent person and that my fears and doubts were only a small part of me. He helped me acquire the confidence and courage to enter nursing school—helped me recognize my potential. We had a good working relationship. I respected his opinion and I believed what he said and, most importantly, he really cared. About me, about all of his patients. I hadn't seen him for a while, so I decided to give him a call.

As I approached his office, I knew what I *wanted* to talk about, but I also knew I just couldn't. Not yet. I started seeing him on a semi-regular basis, about two times a month. We talked again about my childhood, my impending nursing career, my disintegrating marriage. I certainly had enough stuff to keep the sessions going. However, it took me almost a year to mention the house.

During one particular session, while we were sharing stories about our respective vacations, I paused.

"Ron," I hesitatingly stated, "there's something wrong in my house."

"Well, what do you mean, wrong?" he asked.

I started getting very nervous. Although I was extremely comfortable with him and I could talk to him about my most intimate fears and fantasies, this topic still seemed taboo to me. I drew a deep breath and continued. "I think my house is haunted, Ron."

He was very quiet. He sat there and stared at me. Then, after this pause, he simply asked, "Why do you think your house is haunted?" He had an expression of interest on his face, not judgment. I was very grateful for that.

I began to tell him about the suffocating dreams, the feelings of being watched, about what my children, especially Karin, had been going through. Everything. Each statement that flowed out of my mouth was accompanied by an audible sigh of relief. It felt so good.

"I am not very familiar with hauntings," he said, not looking shocked or anything. "I am not even sure what I believe regarding the subject. But, if I were experiencing something unusual in my house, I would look into it. You might want to read some books about other people's experiences with the supernatural, investigate a little. But, whatever you do, don't just assume there is something wrong with you. Your kids and some of your friends and family have noticed something is wrong, too. Trust your feelings. You'll be fine."

He didn't doubt me for a second, didn't doubt my perceptions. That meant a great deal to me. He went on to say he didn't think of me as particularly neurotic and that I needed to listen to my instincts more. "Have faith in yourself," he said. "I do. And let me know what's going on."

His reassurance gave me strength. It gave me a renewed trust in myself, a renewed hope that I could cope with the strange and frightening circumstances in which I found myself, in which my family found themselves. I was determined to hang in there and hope that someday an answer would be found. At the very least, I could stop thinking I was crazy. I thanked him from the bottom of my heart, and left his office feeling light and airy, and bold.

At this point in time, I had graduated, with honors, from nursing school. I was working as a registered nurse in a major metropolitan New York hospital emergency room. I found this section of the hospital to be the most exciting, most challenging. It was one of the places in the hospital where people are at their most vulnerable, their most frightened, and where they are in the most need. I looked forward every day to going to work and helping calm someone's fears. I remember looking at my first evaluation by my supervisors. It said I was: "competent, industrious, and compassionate." Competent, industrious, compassionate. I had fulfilled my dream of becoming a nurse and I was doing well at it. For a person who grew up with so many fears, so many self-doubts, this meant much to me. I felt my self-esteem soar.

I was thirty-eight years old when I completed nursing school, a late bloomer. It had taken me until I was thirty-four to even imagine I could enter nursing school, never mind graduate. But there I was, an ER nurse. I felt so useful, so involved, so "out there," doing my best. Every time I helped someone else be less afraid, I helped myself. The trauma victim, the person having a heart attack, the abused child. Opportunities presented themselves every day, opportunities to make someone's experience in the ER just a little bit better, a little less overwhelming. I loved my job and felt happy at work.

Then I would have to go home. I would have to be in a miserable marriage, in an uncomfortable, frightening house. It was only the smiles on my daughters' faces, the love I felt for them, that kept me going, kept me hoping things would get better.

The house problems were even affecting my job. On those days when I showed up for work tired, not having slept more than an hour or so because of the suffocating dreams, it was difficult to explain why I looked so tired. Some of my colleagues noticed the bags under my eyes.

"You seem to be running on empty," I remember my friend Barbara saying one day.

"Trouble at home, " I told her, not untruthfully. "It's giving me insomnia."

She gave my hand an empathetic squeeze. "Been there," she said.

"Not quite," I thought to myself. Problems with husbands were common among the nurses, especially those who worked in the high-stress environment of the ER. They always assumed any added stress I was under was due to my marriage. I gladly let them think this was the case.

However, I had to do something about my lack of sleep. I only lasted a few months on the day shift, 7:30 A.M. to 4:00 P.M. Not only was my tiredness getting to me, but I worried that I wasn't the best nurse I could be on such little rest. My patients deserved more. I switched to the "graveyard" shift, 11:30 P.M. to 8:00 A.M. It bothered me that the house had forced me to change hours, but, in actuality, it was better for me. On this shift, I could get home in time to bring my daughters to school, get some rest, pick them up at 3:00 P.M. and try to rest again. The suffocating dreams seemed to occur less frequently during the day, and even if they did keep me up, I had another chance to sleep after dinner.

No one at work knew the real reason for my shift change. It didn't seem feasible to tell the truth. Sometimes I would imagine telling one of my fellow nurses something like, "I couldn't sleep last night because I was kept awake by an unseen being pushing me into my bed and making it difficult for me to breathe." I would laugh silently at this thought, knowing for certain those words were in no danger of passing my lips. I imagined someone saying the same thing to me, before all this started, and I would have looked at them as if they were mad. I was happy I kept my mouth shut, but it produced a very lonely, isolated feeling.

My daughters had the advantage of their age. They could mention what was happening to their friends, and it was exciting to them. I wondered, though, about Karin and her suffocating dreams. After she admitted to having them, she didn't mention them very often. She didn't want to talk too much about it, and I didn't know if any of her friends knew of her experiences. Christine had never had one. I was thankful to God for this, but I worried about Karin. Once in a while she would mention having a bad night, but wouldn't elaborate. She did tell me that she would go back to sleep after it was over, something I was not able to do. That might account for her being able to sleep for hours at a time. I was grateful she didn't have to cope with insomnia as well. She also seemed much less frightened than I was, much more able to deal with the situation. I was ashamed that my teenage daughter seemed to demonstrate more courage than me. As far as I was concerned, we seemed to be in a conundrum from which we did not have a way out, that did not fit our view of reality. One that we did not create and did not wish for.

When the feelings of being watched and the suffocating dreams would cease for a while, we would desperately try to pretend that nothing was going on at all. We would embrace the breather, enjoy the vacation. We wouldn't talk about it, wouldn't refer to it, but our hopes were always dashed. Things would start again, usually worse than before.

Karin was in high school, and she started becoming very interested in all forms of animal life. She became one of the coordinators of the animal laboratory at her school. She spent many hours taking care of, and nurturing, monkeys, ducks, rats, gerbils, hamsters, iguanas, and mice. She also developed an avid interest in fish.

We bought her a tank and slowly she managed to accumulate a nice variety of cold-water fish. She diligently took care of them. She changed the water and filter when necessary, fed them on time, and, in general, enjoyed taking great pride in her newly acquired aquatic friends.

One day she came home from school, said her "Hellos" and went downstairs to her room. As soon as she opened her locked door, she let out a screech. I ran downstairs to see what was wrong, and I was shocked. The top of the fish tank had been removed, as well as the charcoal filter. The filter was crushed into her bed, the sheet and bedspread covered with mashed-in charcoal. It was so bizarre. Nothing else was disturbed. No one else had a key to her room. Unless she did this herself, before she went to school, we couldn't figure out how it happened. Something had gotten to the top of the tank, put it aside, grabbed the filter, and done the mashing.

I asked her if she did it.

She looked really hurt when she responded, "No, Mom, I didn't do it!"

She didn't seem to have a motive for doing it. She was more upset about the well-being of her fish than how this had occurred. She ran out and got another filter and installed it immediately. She cared about the fish; as a matter of fact she cared so much about animals that she had recently become a vegetarian. I felt guilty about accusing her, but I didn't have another answer.

The charcoal crushed into the mattress looked very strange. It looked like it was done very much on purpose. It looked like it was done quickly and carelessly. Karin had no explanation. She was frightened, but, again, more concerned about the health of her fish. Again I doubted her, suspected her. I remember thinking what an untrusting mother I was turning out to be. I kept thinking about what I was taught in psychology about how children can act out when they are disturbed about their parents' marriage. I kept blaming myself, my husband, my daughters, for anything unusual happening in our house, except for the suffocating dreams. I knew I needed to stop doing this if I was ever going to get to the truth, but it was so much easier to blame something known, something I could see and touch. I knew I needed to begin to understand that not everything is explainable, and that not everything can be wrapped up in neat, comfortable packages. I knew how lonely I felt, and I thought now about how lonely Karin must have felt. Her own mother didn't believe her.

Other things happened in rapid succession. Karin also had a gerbil cage in her room. It was situated right across from the foot of her bed, on a shelf about two feet from the ceiling. One evening, not long after the fish incident, she awoke to find the gerbil cage hovering right above her head. After floating there for a few moments, it fell on her. She had a visible abrasion on her forehead. She had been alone in her room. She screamed and we ran downstairs. After our hugging her and calming her down, she swore again that it just hovered there, in mid-air, just before it hit her. I was beginning to believe her, remembering the blanket incident, and wondered why she seemed to experience more than the rest of us. I needn't have bothered with this thought because we were soon to catch up.

Not long after the gerbil incident she told me she witnessed something or someone jumping up and down on her bed. She saw dents in her bed and heard the springs, but she didn't actually *see* anyone jumping. She was confused and I was concerned, but the more she reported things like this happening, the more I was inclined to believe her. She didn't seem to profit in any way from these experiences and she seemed so sincere and truthful when she spoke of them. In all other areas, she was doing fine. My ears, and finally, my eyes, were beginning to open wide.

We spoke again about the suffocating dreams. She had them a few nights a week now, sometimes every night, just like me. The respites were getting fewer and farther apart. We all admitted to feeling watched most of the time. If I'd seen this in a movie I would have screamed for the inhabitants of the house to get the hell out of there, but we were actually living this situation. We couldn't so easily leave our home, our only investment. I still hesitated to believe that anything paranormal was actually happening to us. The respites we got went a long way toward convincing us, while they were in effect, that our imaginations were working overtime.

Sometimes I'd fall back into trying to find some reasonable explanation for what was happening to us, especially to Karin. I wanted to believe her, but that belief was a very loaded issue. It proclaimed a reality that I was not willing or ready to accept.

I kept poking and prodding around for some clues as to her emotional state. Was she anxious about anything? Was everything going well at school? Were we paying too much attention to her sister? Freud would have given me an award, but Freud had not experienced our house. Freud would have classified the whole thing as hysteria. He was not as smart as I thought he was.

It was now 1988. Karin was fifteen years old and had inhabited the basement bedroom for two years. Prior to this, although we all experienced funny feelings, hearing footsteps, and we were simultaneously experiencing suffocating dreams, none of us had actually *seen* anything. We had almost gotten used to a sense of being watched and the feeling of foreboding that permeated the house from time to time. Lately, we'd begun to notice a rotting smell coming from below our dining room floor, at the base of a steam pipe. We attributed this to a dead mouse, or an unannounced passing of gas from a family member. The smell would come and go. Sometimes it would change to the distinct smell of freshly cut roses, which put a dent in the "fart" theory! We had no real explanation, so we learned to take these odors in stride and made sure they didn't disturb our daily routine. It amazed even us that a whole family could get used to such an unusual home. We were more understanding of those families we read about, or saw in movies, who did not just run at the first, or second, or third feeling of strangeness in their homes. Denial plows very deeply into our souls. We would rather have a flimsy, semirational explanation, however irrational in reality, than have to deal with the unknown.

Our security in never having actually witnessed anything that could be referred to as ghostly phenomena was very short-lived. Karin began to see what she termed "The Mist." While she was lying in bed, the Mist would drift by her bedroom door. It had an irregular shape to it, was about seven feet tall, and about as wide as an average person. She spoke of it several times and I decided it was time for me to see it myself. I began spending a lot of time in Karin's room. We talked and laughed and I helped her study—all the while watching out for the Mist. She said it came at varying times and she couldn't predict when it would happen. I left my "it must be Karin's imagination" thoughts on the shelf for while and just observed. I wanted to see what she was seeing, if, indeed, she was seeing anything at all. Weeks went by with no sighting. I became a regular in Karin's room, usually while doing the laundry, which Karin's presence made much more tolerable. I nearly forgot about the Mist. I was just enjoying our conversations.

Actually, I had slowly begun to be less fearful and more inquisitive. I so wanted us to be happy in our own home. I wanted to know what was going on. But some of the fear, quite a bit, actually, lingered on. Apparently, I was only capable of taking baby steps in this direction.

One afternoon, another laundry day, I loaded up the washer and Karin and I began to talk about school. She wanted to show me one of her tests, so I went into her room and sat on her bed. We were reviewing her marks when, suddenly, M-ow started to make a strange sound, sort of like a deep growl. She arched her back, hair standing up, like a cat on a Halloween poster. She became very agitated. Within seconds of witnessing M-ow's behavior, I saw the Mist. It was, indeed, just as Karin had described. Amorphous, cloudy, floating past her open door. I was scared. The hairs on my arms were sticking up and I couldn't scream. It was all over in a few seconds. But I saw it, and when I wasn't expecting to. M-ow saw it. The Mist appeared to be a filmy, translucent, gray, quickly moving figure.

My immediate reaction was to hug Karin while M-ow ran after it. We did not go anywhere near the Mist. We stayed on the bed for a few moments longer. Karin was very excited that I'd witnessed this apparition, and so was I. We decided to draw pictures of what we had just seen. We turned our backs on each other and started to draw. The results were strikingly similar. I was spooked beyond belief. Karin just felt vindicated and I didn't blame her. It was about time.

That night I told my husband about what happened and he, as usual, did not believe me. I didn't care about his lack of belief, I just wanted a plumber to come in to see if there was any possibility of condensation existing in that part of the basement. He reluctantly agreed to call one and, a few days later, the basement was examined. No opportunity for condensation was found. The Mist continued to put in appearances in front of my daughter's door, but her fear of it lessened. I, on the other hand, now knowing that there really *was* something down there, experienced a resurgence of my old level of fear. I was even more reluctant to do the laundry without company.

I admired Karin's courage. She was so much more accepting of the possibility that our house was haunted. She even thought it was cool. She simply did not respond with the same level of fear as I did.

When I absolutely insisted Karin stop sleeping in the basement, she became very upset. She saw no reason to give up her privacy—no *reason*. My husband was no help in this area. He didn't believe any of it. Even though he'd had a few of his own experiences, he remained unconvinced that it was anything to be taken seriously. He felt I was overreacting again, and accused me of being overprotective. Karin said she had not been harmed in any way, and she did not expect to be. She seemed to have forgotten about the abrasion from the floating gerbil cage. She didn't care. She was staying put.

For a long time my husband had been promising to move his business out of the top floors so that Karin could move up there, but that couldn't take place for another year or two. Had I been my daughter, I would have "hightailed" it out of that basement ASAP, but she would not budge. If I pleaded with her to stay in the living room, she would simply, as before, wait for me to go to sleep and head on back to her own room. I really didn't want to further infect her with my own fears, so eventually, I stopped barking orders at her to sleep upstairs.

In between sightings of the Mist and the other phenomena, there were still respites. Shorter in duration, but mini-vacations nonetheless. Just enough time would pass to allow us to put some of this stuff out of our minds. Enough time to almost forget. I began to see these brief reprieves as almost cruel in nature. Even when the house was quiet, there was still that awful sense of foreboding. Nothing was actually happening; yet something was there. It was like having the stomach flu. The eventual episode of vomiting was not nearly as bad as the hours of nausea that preceded it. That's what the house felt like at these times. Continuous psychic nausea, knowing the upchucking was coming. In my braver times, I wanted the house to just explode and get it over with. But only in my braver times.

When the mini-vacations were over, incidents would increase. Added to the already disturbing repertoire were sightings of small, shadowy shapes, mostly seen along the baseboards, or moldings, of our home. One night, as I watched television in the living room, I became aware of something moving in the corner of my eye. I turned quickly to my right and saw an amorphous shape, perhaps only a foot in height, with no discernable width. It was hard to see where it started or ended. The borders were hazy at best and the color was a sort of slate brown to black. Karin and Christine were with me, and I asked them if they saw anything, without describing it to them. They saw it.

Christine said, very maturely, "Mom, that looks like a rolled-up blanket, only cloudy. What is it?"

Karin perked up, too. She was amazed that they didn't disappear when they were stared at. They would linger for a while, then scurry away, then return.

"Did you see that, Mom? This is unreal—let's go over to them," Karin suggested.

"No way," was my predictable response.

They came and went, slowly moving away from us, never toward us. The only good thing about these curious shapes was that they were not threatening in any way. They did not produce any fear. Actually, they seemed to engender a feeling of sadness. We found ourselves feeling sorry for them. They became regular visitors to our house.

These unnamed shapes had no rhyme or reason to their appearances, or their disappearances. Weeks would go by without seeing them, and then there they'd be, down by the baseboards of our dining room, living room, or hallway. To my knowledge, they were never spotted in the basement, my bedroom or Christine's, or the kitchen or bathroom. They seemed to like just those limited areas of our house.

After a while, their presence did not evoke any sort of unusual response. We just verbally acknowledged them and went about our business. I wondered always what or who they were, and what they wanted from us, if anything. They were very unintrusive and I found myself wishing they were the only anomalies present in our home. I could handle them with no trouble at all and was perfectly willing to share our living space with them. I was very proud of how we adapted to these strange and mystifying apparitions.

However, within a few months, another form of something unexplainable presented itself to us. This took the form of balls of light. We first spotted them one evening as Karin, Christine, and I were gathered in the living room, once again watching TV. I was lying flat on my stomach, propping my head up by leaning my jaw on my hands. In this position I could see the hallway with the stairs leading to the second floor. I noticed a stream of light come from the hallway, enter the living room at the top of the ceiling, and whiz through to the dining room. My first thought was that the light must have been a reflection on my eyeglasses. The light stopped and I tried to recreate it by moving my glasses in all sorts of directions, but I couldn't. I dismissed the light and continued to watch television. A few moments later, it happened again, but this time I got a better look at it. It was a ball of light, about the size of a ping-pong ball, close to the ceiling. It had a halo not unlike the one on a star drawn on a Christmas card when the artist wants to show it twinkling. It also looked like a camera's flashbulb when it just popped, only the popping effect was steady, not pulsating. I stared at it and watched it move, once again, from the hallway into the living room, then into the dining room, and then it disappeared. I turned to my children with, I'm sure, a look of astonishment on my face.

"Did you see that?" I asked.

Karin and Christine were both laughing. "Sure we saw that, Mom. We've been seeing these things for weeks now," said a giggling Christine.

Karin nodded in agreement. "We've been seeing them all over the house and were just waiting for you to see them too. Aren't they something? They never move from the ceiling, no matter what room they're in. Look, here comes another one."

And there it was. Just like the one before it. They made no sound whatsoever. They moved very fast and there didn't seem to be any real substance to them. They didn't generate any perceptible heat or coldness, nor did they cause any fear.

After my first sighting, or my initiation, as my daughters like to call it, I saw them all the time. It was as if once my mind was open to seeing something I could no longer not see it. Sometimes during dinner, even when my husband was present, these lights would just come zooming around the dining room ceiling. They'd dance about for a while, perhaps a few seconds, and then they'd disappear. My husband never saw them, or at least, he never admitted to it. My children and I had yet another thing to share a private laugh about. The whole picture was really not so funny.

It just boggled my mind that now we were being required, by the house, to deal with not only all the other uncomfortable phenomena, but also the shapes that hugged our baseboards and these incredible balls of light. I couldn't help but wonder what would be next. I was grateful that these new visitors were not threatening, but I still was frightened as to what might occur in the future.

A few mornings later, while I was opening up my mail, I noticed a brochure from the local community college. I browsed through the classes, briefly reminiscing as I came to their nursing program, when I noticed an ad for a class on parapsychology.

It was called "Studies in the Paranormal," and it was an accepted, three-credit course in the psychology department. I called the school immediately, readmitted myself, and enrolled the following week. I was so excited by the possibility of learning more about what was happening to us, about perhaps even getting some answers.

I had to wait two weeks for the class to start and I felt like a kid waiting for a present to arrive.

4 It was wonderful being back on the campus of Kingsborough Community College. It is located in the Manhattan Beach section of Brooklyn, right on the shores of the Atlantic Ocean. The campus is sprawling, with many different kinds of trees and flowers, and the architecture is a marvelous blend of modern and Aztec-like buildings. It was built in 1963 and is still in very good condition, with no graffiti on the buildings, no litter on the grounds. I enjoyed driving through the entrance so much, mostly because it brought back memories of nursing school. With the exception of the birth of my two children, nursing school was the best experience of my life.

As I made my way to class, I passed so many places that stirred up pleasant recollections. I think the fondness in my heart for my nursing classes was due mostly to the fact that it was my first venture into life outside my marriage. For the first time I was accomplishing something on my very own, and doing well at it. As I passed the on-campus theater, I couldn't help but remember the day I gave my valedictorian address to my graduating class. It was such a high point in my life. It was in this state of mind that I entered my new classroom.

I had stopped by the bookstore to purchase a new book, and of course, a new pen, and I was fiddling with these things as I got settled in. The students streamed in and I found myself looking them over in great detail. I wondered who among them was experiencing any of the same phenomena I was. And I wondered who was here just for the three credits. I didn't know what I was expecting, but no one looked particularly different or outstanding, so I just concentrated on waiting for the teacher to arrive.

Dr. Phil Stander entered the room. He was a man of average height, with a receding hairline and a pleasant smile, and wearing an outrageous tie. During the course of the semester, I noticed he wore a different, outlandish tie for every class. It made him seem sort of interesting to me. I wondered why he picked such wild colors and incredible prints—flowers, microchips, boxes, abstract designs. Those ties really added some color to the otherwise dreary-looking classroom.

He was very soft-spoken, but any fear I had of his lectures being boring was quickly replaced with a fascination for the subject matter. He spoke of the paranormal as if it was an everyday fact of life. To him, hauntings and poltergeists were commonplace and something to be investigated, not feared. I listened with interest to what he had to say, and when class was dismissed I went to the bookstore to purchase our textbook for the semester, *Esp, Hauntings and Poltergeists: A Parapsychologist's Handbook,* written by Loyd Auerbach. I loved the title. It made the subject seem so scientific, and I started reading as soon as I arrived home.

The class met twice a week and mostly consisted of a brief lecture followed by class discussion. The topics included psychic ability, ghosts, hauntings, ESP, automatic writing, and poltergeists. I was not familiar with most of these subjects, so I kept quiet most of the time. This was unusual for me. As a student, I normally liked to sit front row center, and speak up very frequently, but in this case I felt intimidated by my lack of knowledge. I sat in the back and observed. I wasn't sure what to make of what I was hearing.

We all took notes while Dr. Stander started defining terms, "From what we know, we can, with a certain amount of clarity and exactness, describe a few phenomena. Poltergeists are noisy, disruptive spirits. They can move furniture or other objects around, or just be noisy most of the time. Poltergeists are usually associated with the presence in the house of an adolescent, or preadolescent child. We are not sure what the connection is, but we know it exists. Hauntings are apparitions that appear on a regular basis, at the same time, and same place, doing the same thing. We like to think of them as a recording of a past event, usually traumatic, that is replayed back on some sort of psychic tape. Apparitions, or ghosts, on the other hand, may move about freely and try, or not try, to interact with whomever it comes in contact with."

He paused to allow us time to copy what he said, then he continued, "Then there is ESP, or extrasensory perception. This includes telepathy: the ability to know what is in another person's thoughts; precognition: the ability to receive information about the future; and clairvoyance: knowing information about objects or events by psychic, not normal, means."

He went on and on like this. At first I copied down every word. I began to get a little tired, though, not from the writing, but from not hearing anything similar to what was happening to myself and my family. At any other time, I would have embraced all the information being shot at me, but at that moment I wanted relief so badly. I wanted to hear that balls of light and strange shapes were nothing to worry about. Mostly, I wanted someone to mention anything that sounded like a suffocating dream to me.

I studied all the different terms, and passed the written tests, but I had a lot of questions and was not quite sure how to ask them. I was reading the textbook at home, but had not gotten too far into it yet.

During one very enjoyable class, Dr. Stander gave us a "psychic test." He used cards with different designs on them and we were supposed to guess which design was next, before it was shown to us. I failed so miserably. While I was doing it, I was sure I got most of them right and I was very disappointed at how bad I actually did. He also gave us a test to determine our ability to perceive the paranormal, and, again, I failed. I was happy these tests were not in any way pertinent to our final grade.

During this class, I began to notice two women, sitting a few aisles away from me. They wore their curly black hair long, and were adorned with a lot of silver jewelry. I admired their jewelry because I have always loved sterling silver. On the whole I thought they looked very interesting, if a bit witchy. They always seemed to have something to say and they laughed a lot during class. Ordinarily, I would have joined them, but I just did not seem like my usual student-self in this class.

At home, in the evenings, I continued to read the textbook. Mr. Auerbach's book did not contain a section on balls of light or suffocating dreams, and I didn't know what category they were in, so I had to be content with reading the whole book, which was full of facts and information on so many aspects of the paranormal. It was very well written, certainly covered a lot of ground, and it addressed both skeptics and believers. I was most interested in what he had to say about poltergeists.

According to Mr. Auerbach, "The word 'poltergeist' means 'noisy ghost' and is generally used when objects (such as pictures on the wall, knickknacks on the shelf, utensils in the kitchen, furniture) seemingly float or fly around the house, or appliances or lights turn themselves on and off, with occasional unusual sounds (like rappings or footsteps) or smells or even images experienced. Until the twentieth century, the typical interpretation of the poltergeist experience was one involving mischievous spirits of the dead. However, as more and more cases were looked into, as our investigative models for psychic functioning in the living came into better focus (especially ideas of mind influencing matter), parapsychologists were better able to understand just what was happening. The conception of the poltergeist as somehow related to a human agent, a person (or persons) living or working in the situation came into being, and currently this is the main model that we work with."

I found this and other descriptions of poltergeists in his book very disturbing. I wondered if someone in my house, including myself, could be causing subconsciously the experiences we were having, even without intent. I found myself reviewing much of what had happened to us. I wasn't sure at all if we fit into this, or any other category.

It did not explain my brother's sense of foreboding the first time he entered our house. Nor did it explain why the phenomena happened whether one of us, or all of us, were at home. It never mentioned anything about balls of light or those scurrying shapes, but I did think of the time Karin's sheets were taken off her bed, in my presence, and the gerbil incident, and the fish tank charcoal filter. I was very confused and still more than a bit frightened. I wanted very much to speak to Dr. Stander in private, but I just didn't have the courage.

As I read on further, Mr. Auerbach mentioned many cases of psychic phenomena involving apparitions and ghosts, some only slightly resembling what was going on with us. As far as I could ascertain, we seemed to have some sort of mixture of phenomena, none of which was explained in detail in the book. The one thing I am sorry I read was his reference to the movie *The Entity*. I had seen that movie a few years ago and it frightened me so much I would not allow the video in my home. I thought of our suffocating dreams and I had been scared half out of my mind that they might accelerate into the sexual attacks this woman apparently experienced.

I was grateful that Mr. Auerbach explained that the movie greatly exaggerated this woman's encounters. Something definitely happened to her, and evidently continues to happen to her, but not what we saw in the movie. Still, just the mention of *The Entity* made me put the book down for a few days.

As enlightening as this book was about so many different areas of psychic research and investigation, I still found most of my questions unanswered. Whenever Dr. Stander gave us the opportunity to stand up in class, I declined to do so. Most of the other students did not have much to offer in the way of experiences, and some of them took this whole subject as a joke. However, those two women I mentioned earlier stood up together one day and spoke, very calmly, about what had happened to them in a house they shared. They said they'd seen "small, cloudy shapes, low to the ground," and they also gave a description of light balls that sounded very close to ours. They mentioned, almost matter of factly, that they felt watched most of the time they were in their home. They had moved out after a few years and had been quite comfortable since.

What amazed me the most about their speech was the fact that they were not afraid of what happened to them, and had not been afraid even while it was happening. They said they just figured some restless spirit had been visiting them and they had no desire to get rid of it. I wanted so much to ask them if their sleep was ever interrupted, but I didn't. I decided that since I was most comfortable writing my feelings down, I would, toward the end of the term, write a letter to Dr. Stander.

I continued to enjoy the class, and, once or twice, I brought my daughters with me.

They were thrilled to learn that some of the phenomena had actual names, that people were studying these things and that other people had experienced, if not the same thing, then at least something close. On one of the days that my daughters were there, Dr. Stander happened to comment on what those two women had spoken of. He maintained that light balls were "discarnate spirits—spirits without a body," and that the small, dark shapes they had seen were different representations of the same thing. These spirits simply had not "gone on to the light." For a few moments, we felt validated, and that was such a good feeling. It wasn't a complete explanation, but at least it was something.

The last week of class, Dr. Stander assigned us a term paper, and he left the subject matter up to each student, as long as it pertained to our class. That's when I decided I would pour my heart out and explain to him what had been happening to us.

My term paper was very long, much longer than he had required. In it, I described, in detail and as best as I could, everything that had happened in our house. I was not prepared for his response.

On the last day of class, he handed back the papers, and the student in me was thrilled to have received an "A". However, he asked that I wait until everyone else was gone because he wanted to speak to me privately. I went back to my seat and waited until we were alone. He was absolutely excited about what he'd read in my paper.

"Elaine, I want to study your whole family. I want to do interviews and visit your house. I'm writing a book on psychic phenomena and your house is just what I've been looking for. I can't wait to get some equipment in there, and talk to your daughters and their friends and everyone who has had an experience in your home. When can I interview your daughters?"

I didn't know what to say. As happy as I was that he was interested, I found the idea of someone studying my family and my home very intrusive. I did, however, agree to go with my daughters to his office for an initial interview.

On the day of the interview, Karin had to be in school for a test, so just Christine and I went. She was so excited—very willing to tell this man everything she'd witnessed. She responded to his questions as honestly as she could. She mentioned the noises, the balls of light, the shadowy shapes. She hadn't seen the Mist or had a suffocating dream so she didn't talk about these things. She described her experiences exactly as I had in my term paper. She hadn't even read it. Dr. Stander was impressed. He was writing so fast, and so happily, he seemed almost like a child himself.

However, Christine reacted to the phenomena very much like I did. She was frightened, she wanted it to go away, and she was very uncomfortable living with it. As the interview wore on, I noticed Christine getting somewhat nervous. Some of Dr. Stander's questions were disquieting and intrusive, especially for a ten-year-old.

"How do you feel when you see the balls of light?" he asked. "Do you get scared? Are you afraid at night? What do your friends think about your house? What does that rotting smell in the dining room make you think of? Are you afraid of ghosts?"

I could see Christine start to squirm in her seat. As happy as she was when we walked in, she was no longer thrilled to be there. She looked frightened to me. I wanted it stopped. "We've got to go, Dr. Stander," I said as I got our things together, "I'm feeling very uncomfortable about this."

"Well, that's okay for now, but we have only just started. I want you to know this was just the beginning. I plan on doing at least 125 interviews and a full-scale investigation."

One hundred and twenty-five interviews! I became a little agitated at this thought and I told him so.

"This is not the way we want to handle the problem. I am not at ease talking this way, and I don't think my daughter is either."

Christine nodded in agreement.

"I think we're going to go home now and I'll call you if we change our minds. I had no idea you wanted to do so many interviews. I don't know what exactly I was expecting, but I wasn't ready for this. I just want our phenomena to go away. I don't want us to be looked at under a microscope. I don't want us to become some sort of media event, with strangers poking and prodding around my house. There has to be a better way."

He seemed so disappointed. I think he meant well, but I also think he was looking very hard for material for his upcoming book. I promised I'd call if I had a change of heart, but I knew I wouldn't. The interview had made everything seem so real, so much more frightening. Just his questions were enough to produce a sick feeling inside the pit of my stomach. I took Christine by the hand and left his office.

As I was driving home, I asked myself why I had gotten so upset. I certainly didn't like putting Christine through such intense questioning, but it was more than that. I truly didn't want strangers in my house, examining us. But it was still more than that. I think I was afraid of what they would find. I knew something was there and I wasn't at all sure I wanted to find out what it was. I was afraid they would stir things up. I clung to the fantasy that if I left things alone, it would not get any worse. Again, I was wrong.

5 My studies in the paranormal were somewhat enlightening, but my refusal to be interrogated by my professor left me with the feeling that there might be no way to resolve the problem plaguing my house. I was glad to have read about other people in similar circumstances, but in each story I found so much that was not related to what we were experiencing. We had such a "mix" of things in the house, such a jumble of seemingly disconnected phenomena.

About a month after my class ended, the phenomena started to increase again. The unseen footsteps became louder and we began hearing muffled voices during the day and night. These voices were quite disturbing. They sounded like male voices, like a group of men talking at a distance, none of their words being intelligible. At first we thought the voices came from outside, but when we looked, there were never any men gathered near our house. We checked to see if a radio or TV had been left on, we even checked to see if maybe someone had left a cassette in the stereo system. We heard these voices when we were all together and we had each heard them separately. They were heard with no predictability, never at a certain time or in a particular place.

Karin had become even more uncomfortable, almost alarmed at times. I was very happy when, on her own, without any nagging from me, she began sleeping almost every night on the upstairs couch. I felt better knowing she wasn't alone downstairs. The basement was feeling more and more "inhabited." Even when someone was with me while I did the laundry, I couldn't shake the feeling of fear in my solar plexus. I started hating my formerly prized washer and dryer, and would put off washing clothes for as long as possible. I actually longed to go the the laundromat, and sometimes I did just that! I felt so ludicrous lugging a week's worth of laundry down the block, spending half a day in the steamy laundromat. I remember sitting there, trying, but unable, to read a magazine. I just couldn't concentrate on anything. Every time I put coins into the washer or dryer, I felt so foolish—sometimes foolish enough to cry.

I was thrilled when my husband decided to move his business from the upper two floors of our house to a new location, about four miles away. We could have rented the upstairs apartment, but I was anxious to get Karin out of the basement bedroom. We gave her the three rooms on the third floor, in the attic. Two of the rooms were quite small, but the front room, where she would sleep, was a nice size. That's where the previous owners, the old man's nephew and his wife, had their bedroom, and it was also the room with the wide picture window overlooking our beautiful tree. For a high school student, it was a perfect place to study and have privacy. She had enough room, and then some, for her fish and gerbils. Enough room for a desk and a love seat and even a place for storage. Since my husband had employed four or five people who used to go up to the attic for supplies, and not one of them had ever reported any unusual disturbances, I figured it was a good bet there would be no problem with spirits there.

On some level, I think I understood that this thought was irrational, but I longed for Karin to sleep in a safe place. I was trying very hard to make sense out of nonsense and to feel in some sort of control. I was excited and happy that, perhaps, once the basement was vacated, our troubles would be over.

Shortly before Karin moved all her belongings up to the attic, she and her best friend, Maria, were in her basement bedroom playing a game when they heard the front door open and heard footsteps leading to the top of the basement stairs. I was at work and Christine was at her grandparent's house. My husband was on a business trip and no one else was in the house. The two upper floors were now empty. They became scared and ran out of the house and down the block to where Maria lived.

They asked Maria's father to check out our house. When they'd left, all the lights were shut off, except for the basement light and the light in our living room. They had locked the doors behind them. Karin gave Maria's father the keys and he came over only a minute or two later, but the doors were now unlocked, and every light in the house was on. *Every* light. Three floors of lights. Lamps, ceiling lights, night lights, outside lights. He checked the house, and, after making sure there were no intruders, he turned everything off, except for the light over the front door. He also locked the doors when he left.

He went back to his house, where Karin and Maria were waiting, and told them everything was okay. By the time they came back to our house, the door was once again unlocked and all the lights were on again. Too embarrassed to call Maria's father again, they simply waited on the front steps for me to come home. When I arrived, an hour or so later, they were still shaking. My brother, Joe, happened to be staying at my parents' house that night, and since they live only a few blocks away, I called and had him come over and recheck the house. He found nothing. I went back to my parents' with my brother to pick up Christine and returned home and immediately telephoned Maria's dad. His name was also Joe.

"Hi, Joe, this is Elaine. The girls are still here and I was wondering if you could tell me what happened this evening. They are really upset. You came over before? What did you see?"

"Oh, yeah," he replied. "You should have seen them earlier. They ran over here like they'd seen a ghost. You know how kids are, but I went over to your house and checked anyway. By the way, you shouldn't leave all those lights on, I mean, it can get very expensive, you know? I didn't find anything wrong, but they insisted they heard someone come in the front door when they were downstairs. They have such imaginations at their age."

I didn't question him further. I knew he wouldn't be receptive to what I would have liked to ask. I just thanked him for coming over and turned my attention to the kids. Karin and Maria were still very shaken. They were both occupied telling

Christine all about what happened. As I listened again to their story, I started to feel a sense of sadness. I hated the fact that they had gotten so scared, and I hadn't been around to help them. And I hated the fact that now we had the additional symptom of lights going on and off without logical explanation.

That night, after Maria went home, Karin, Christine, and I slept together in the living room, with all the lights on. We didn't know what to be more afraid of, that an actual person had entered our house and was playing games with us, or unknown forces were responsible for the footsteps and lights and locked and unlocked doors. We felt terribly spooked. We huddled there, watching TV, until we fell asleep. I thought of driving all of us to my parent's house for the night, but I hesitated. I didn't want to start that. Running there had the connotation that we were no longer capable of dealing with this on our own. I wasn't ready for that admission. Not yet, anyway.

We felt a little safer knowing that my husband would be coming home from his trip in the early morning hours. When he arrived, about 5 A.M., his keys in the door woke me up. He was surprised to see us all sleeping together. "What the hell are you all doing in the living room at this hour?" he said, flipping his attaché case on the dining room table.

I related to him what had happened the night before, but as usual he wasn't very impressed. With a look of condescension, he offered his opinion. "The fuse box probably shorted out. You guys are getting upset over nothing. I really wish you'd just forget about all this bullshit."

With a dismissive wave of his hand, he left me in the living room and went to bed. Instead of getting angry at him, I decided I liked his explanation. I didn't like the *way* he said it, but I liked it nevertheless. It made so much more sense and was so much less frightening than my interpretation of what happened. I was more than willing to push aside the forgotten locked and unlocked doors. So were my children. I glanced over at them lying on the floor, peering out at me through bundles of quilts, nodding their heads in agreement. They looked so unbelievably sweet.

It took two or three weeks to move all of my husband's business things out of the upper floors. Desks, lamps, photocopy machines, telephones. Soon the rooms were empty and we started making plans to move Karin into her new space. On the second, or middle floor, where most of his office had been located, was now to be a playroom in the back, a kitchen/dining room in the middle and an "extra" bedroom in the front. It wasn't long before my husband would make full use of this "extra" room. He moved himself up there about a month later and, for the last three years of our marriage, we slept on separate floors. I looked at it as the relationship equivalent of training wheels on a bicycle. I was learning to sleep without him. Eventually I would learn to live without him.

Regardless of the implications of the impending new sleeping arrangements, it was sort of fun rearranging the whole house. The basement would soon be empty, except, of course, for the washer and dryer. We were even clearing out the "den" area. We realized no one ever went down there to watch TV anyway. The three rooms in the attic were officially Karin's. My husband only had a few more things to move out and then the middle floor would be empty too. During the weekdays, when Karin was at school, no one was upstairs at all.

My husband chose a holiday Monday, I believe it was President's day, to move out the last of his equipment. He was finished by about 10 A.M. and left to start his first day at the new office. Karin was asleep on the living room couch, Christine was in her bedroom, and I in mine. We were all suddenly awakened by a very loud sound. It was as if someone had dropped a very heavy piece of furniture. My first thought was that perhaps workers were doing some construction on our block. We all got up and looked outside. No construction. We heard it a few more times, so we got together in the dining room and tried to focus on where the sound was coming from. It was quiet. A few minutes passed.

Then, *bang . . . bang . . . bang . . .* right over our heads. Upstairs. Like someone stomping their foot, but many times louder, heavier. The sound moved through the whole middle floor. We could hear it banging from the front of the house, then the middle, then the back. Whenever it reached the middle, above the dining room where we were huddled, the ceiling fixture seemed to vibrate. We started timing it. Every five or six minutes it would start all over again. I put in an urgent call to my husband and asked him to come home. He was really pissed off, but he said he'd come. We waited for him, all of us sitting on the front steps. The noise was even audible from the outside of the house.

As I waited with my children that wintry day, I realized that it bothered me to always be calling a male whenever we got frightened. In this day and age of enlightenment as far as women are concerned, and thinking of myself as pretty much liberated, it embarrassed me quite a bit to realize that, in times of fear, I ran to a man. It upset me even further to recognize that this was, indeed, my absolute gut reaction. At those times I simply did not want one of my female friends to come over. I wanted my husband, or my brother, or my father—even a male neighbor. Having a male around made me feel safer, more secure. More importantly, it made me feel protected.

I felt like I had to be the protector of my children, but I wanted someone to protect me, too. It was disturbing to me that in other aspects of my life I considered myself as growing more and more independent—as a parent, at work, in my marriage, but when it came to dealing with particularly frightening times in the house, I felt almost childlike when it came to the level of fear I would experience. It disturbed me the most when it was my husband to whom I turned for protection. I didn't want him to play that role for me in that way. Although financially I guess I was, in a way, protected by him, I certainly didn't feel that way in any other sense. My train of thought on this matter ended here as I breathed a begrudging sigh of relief when I heard the angry "honk, honk" of his car horn.

He quickly exited his car and shouted, "What is it now? I was busy at work and you just had to call. What's wrong this time?"

"I'm sorry I bothered you, I know it's your first day at the new office, but, there was this sound. We all heard it. Come inside and listen." I was really scared he'd just leave, but he didn't. Actually, he started to get back in his car, but I wouldn't let him.

"Please, please, just come inside for a few minutes," I cried. "You can even hear it out here if you don't want to come in the house." But he did come in. And we waited.

Nothing happened. He began to look at us as if we really were crazy. Then, about fifteen minutes after his arrival, it began, even louder than before. *Bang . . . bang . . . bang.* My husband seemed absolutely shocked.

"What the hell is that?" he exclaimed. "It's so loud. There's got to be a logical explanation for it."

I hoped he was right.

We were sitting in the living room when it started again, and he could tell it was clearly coming from the second floor. I must admit I took a certain sort of pleasure in seeing him perplexed. I sort of smiled inside when I said those most popular and sought-after words, "See, I told you so. I told you we heard something."

We just stood in the living room and listened. A few minutes later, the banging came again. My husband put his finger to his lips as if to make the "shoosh" sound and he silently directed us to go upstairs. We all walked up the stairs in unison, my husband leading the pack. Karin and Christine seemed very brave and willing to go up there now that their father was home.

The way we were walking upstairs, given another scenario, was quite amusing. It looked like we were all attached, inching our way up the stairs. My husband went first, with Karin and Christine in the middle, and myself in the back.

We went through all the rooms, even the bathroom. We saw nothing, and, exasperatingly, heard nothing, the whole time we were up there. We relaxed a little, we talked, and we waited. Nothing. My husband was understandably anxious to return to work, so, after about fifteen minutes, we went back downstairs. As I was saying "Goodbye" to him, it happened again.

He turned toward the staircase and just exclaimed "I can't believe this. What in the hell is going on here?" He came back inside, sat in the living room with us, and waited some more. During this time the episodes of banging repeated themselves in groups of three "bangs," followed by a few minutes of silence. We had no explanation whatsoever.

He really had to get back to work, so he left, and my daughters and I decided we did not want to go back into the house. I ran back inside for a few moments to get my pocketbook and then we went out to lunch and did some shopping. By the time we returned, it was past our dinner hour and my husband was at home, watching television.

While I was cooking dinner, the banging happened a few more times, and then stopped. It never happened again.

"I can't explain today at all," my husband offered, "but that doesn't mean I believe all the other things you guys tell me. But, Elaine, I have had some nasty experiences since I've been sleeping on the second floor. That bedroom seems weird sometimes. After I fall asleep, perhaps a few hours later, I wake up and can't seem to move.

"It's like I'm paralyzed in the bed and the pressure on my chest is really heavy. The first time it happened I thought I was having a heart attack or something. But I wasn't. After a few minutes, the feeling leaves and I am okay again. Also, one night, about a week ago, I saw a dark figure, very menacing, approaching my bed. It was cloudy and sort of blackish, but when I sat up, it went away. Actually, it went out the doors and onto the terrace. But, and I really mean this, I still don't think this house is haunted. I don't know what's going on, but whatever it is can certainly be explained."

"Well, explain it then," I said. "Go ahead. I'd really like to hear it."

He said nothing further, just walked upstairs to his new bedroom and left us downstairs to ponder what this might be all about. We didn't know any more than he did.

A few days later, one evening when my husband was working late, the girls and I were downstairs watching TV when we started hearing the photocopy machine upstairs making its familiar sound, the sound these machines make when they are in the process of copying something. It is very distinct and very identifiable.

Having had my husband's office upstairs for such a long time, we were very used to this particular sound, and, initially, thought nothing of it. However, we soon realized that there was no photocopy machine up there any longer. We stood at the bottom of the stairs listening to a machine that no longer existed. This did not happen for a few minutes. It happened for a few hours. None of us ventured upstairs to see what was going on. I didn't call my husband this time. We just went back to watching TV. We had no explanation, we did not want to explore the possibilities. We simply wanted it to go away.

Karin, however, did offer a curious thought. "Maybe, just maybe," she said, "we've always heard this sound and just naturally attributed it to the photocopy machine because we knew one was up there."

It was an interesting thought. However, this sound diminished as time went by, and within a month or two we never heard it again.

I had the distinct feeling that the house might, in some way, have the capability to reproduce sounds that once existed within its walls.

Thinking about the banging and the photocopy machine sounds made me wonder if someone or something, or maybe spirits were trying to communicate with us, why in this way? I couldn't figure out what they wanted or what they were trying to say. I couldn't understand what these sounds represented or how we were ever going to figure this out.

A few weeks of quiet followed this episode, then something very bizarre happened to Christine. She was in the sixth grade and doing rather well at the time. Although she could become frightened during the active phases of our house, she easily returned to her outgoing, friendly self once things settled again. We talked a lot about what was happening. I didn't hide my bewilderment or fear, and I think this helped her to more easily admit hers. When she was frightened, we always stayed in the same room together, even if it was all through the night. I knew she talked to her friends about the house—unlike me, she had no trouble doing this. I think it made her feel better. And eleven-year-olds are so much more open-minded than adults. She said no one made fun of her or ridiculed her. They thought it was interesting. Some of them even wanted to sleep over just to see if anything happened!

I wasn't very worried about her. Up until this point, except for reporting hearing those muffled male voices, she had only experienced strange things when someone else was with her. Never when she was alone. Perhaps that's why, even when she was frightened, she never seemed overwhelmingly so.

Her own personal experiences started one balmy spring evening. She was in the dining room on the first floor, doing her homework. I was in the kitchen, cooking dinner. We were separated by the dining room wall. All of a sudden I heard her scream. I ran into the dining room and saw her crying.

"My, God, Christine, what happened?" I asked, really worried about her. She was not the type of child who screamed for no reason.

"Mommy," she sobbed, "I was reading my math book when someone threw water on me. Look at my shirt!"

The back of her white shirt was really wet. She was shaking and crying. As I held her to me, I looked around. There was no source of water in the dining room. We had no sprinkler system in there, no refrigerator, no leaky or exposed pipes. Karin wasn't home. No friends were visiting. I could not understand how her back could get wet like that. She wasn't sweating anywhere on her body. She had no water gun, and, even if she did, how would she point it at her own back?

Thoughts like these raced through my mind as I held her until she stopped crying.

"I'm scared, Mommy. Why did they shoot me with water?" she cried.

Why, indeed, I thought. She joined me in the kitchen, and after she calmed down we had a good talk. I wanted to know how she felt about what her sister had been experiencing and what we'd all heard and seen at times. She was very honest with me, I think.

"Sometimes, Mommy, I get really scared," she said, "but only sometimes. I think Karin is very brave and I wish you wouldn't get so upset about our ghosts. Ghosts are okay as long as they don't hurt anyone. Why are you so scared of them?"

I truly didn't know what to say to her. I didn't want her to catch my level of fear, nor did I want to make believe nothing was happening. So I said, "Chris, I just feel real uncomfortable not knowing what is causing the things that are happening to us. I want some answers and I don't know how to get them."

She looked at me all wide-eyed and beautiful. "Maybe, Mommy, we have to wait for the answers."

All I could think of was part of the old quotation: "From the mouths of babes." I thought her comment was so smart, and I told her so. She beamed at my compliment and offered her wonderful child-arms out for a hug. As we embraced, I told her, "I'm sorry, sweetheart, that we seem to be living in a haunted house. Do you want to move?"

She looked up at me, her eyes still wet from tears,"Yeah, Mommy, sometimes I really would like to move. But not all the time. I don't think the ghosts want to hurt me, but I got really scared today. I don't know why, but I feel so sorry for them. I feel like they're crying most of the time. I don't hear them, but I still think that. Maybe we should try to help them. Could we, Mom, could we help them?"

Her compassion for something that had just frightened her overwhelmed me. Once again, my fear was worse than hers. Now I felt ashamed that I was even more upset than my *youngest* child. I had begun this conversation with Christine with the intent of comforting her and ended it with a feeling that what she was most concerned about was comforting them. I felt myself growing more and more tired of the whole situation. I thought it was awful that my children had actually gotten *used* to the strange goings on in our home, and I was not at all sure this was a good thing. I felt guilty that I didn't seem capable of protecting them in this situation, and I was afraid I'd already let it go too far. I was terrified that Christine would start to experience those suffocating dreams. I got really scared that day, in a way I had not been before. I did not want to ask any more questions. I wanted to get out, I wanted to move, and I wanted to move as soon as possible.

I waited for my husband to come home from work and, with a forced smile on my face, I broached the subject that I knew would get him upset. "I need to talk about this house. Please, we have got to get out of here. We've got to move. Now. I don't care about the investment. We could sell the house and get another one. We could move into my parent's house, or maybe an apartment, if we can't sell the house."

At this point, I was really crying. "We can't stay here. We can't let the kids stay here. Enough is enough." I shook while I waited for his response.

"I can't believe you're starting this shit again, Elaine," he said, slowly taking off his coat. "I don't want to move and, even if I did, there is simply no reason to sell this house. It's big enough for all of us, we worked hard on it, and," he continued, his frustration building, "and . . . and . . . *whatever* . . . we are most definitely not selling this house! If you were not so goddamn hysterical about everything, so ridiculous with all this haunting crap, the kids wouldn't blink an eye. So big deal, a few weird things happened. So what. You don't go selling a house because of it. That's it. Case closed."

I felt so powerless. We co-owned the house and not a penny of anything else was in my name. He ran the bank accounts, he ran all the finances. I had no credit cards in my name, no checking account. I only had a few hundred dollars saved. My mind just began racing. In reality, I knew I couldn't move in with my parents because they had no room for us. Likewise with my brother. He lived in a studio apartment in Manhattan. And even if I temporarily moved in with him, I knew the kids had to go to school and they couldn't go to school from Manhattan. I was really getting panicky. I even thought of going to a motel with the girls, and that thought just made the feeling of being trapped worse. I wasn't brave enough to just move us all out of there on my own. And how long would we have to stay there? I was stuck, and I hated it.

I was so upset that I called in sick to work for a few days. I felt I needed some time to myself, just to think of a way out. At the end of my self-induced vacation all I could come up with was to simply go on. I was terribly angry at my husband, at his inability to even try to see what was going on in the house. He left for work early in the morning and didn't come back home until evening. Even when he had worked upstairs, he had traveled around and kept himself very busy. He refused to believe that anything was wrong. He made up all sorts of excuses for his own suffocating dreams, and denigrated any and all of our other experiences. I fantasized, with pleasure, of pots and pans jumping out of our closets and hitting him smack in the head. In my mind I saw him turning around, astonished, with me standing by him with an all-knowing smile on my face. It was a wonderful fantasy, but that was all it was.

I decided that, since I couldn't seem to remove us from this situation, then perhaps I could learn to look at things a little differently. I knew my fear level was higher than that of both my daughters and I wondered if the fear itself prevented me from trying to better understand what was really going on. I could even appreciate the mystery we had here and, if I could just calm down a little, maybe I could figure out a better way to deal with the whole thing. I knew, for sure, that I could no longer go to one of those scary movies and scream for the inhabitants to run out of their house.

I could no longer criticize the plot for having the actors behave so stupidly. There I was, just like my on-screen counterparts, continuing to live in an uncomfortable, frightening situation. Life imitates art, I thought. I also knew, for sure, that I had to do something. Exactly what that was, I did not know.

One other "water" incident happened to Christine about a month later. Once again she was in the dining room doing her homework and was splashed, on the back, just like before. She wasn't as upset at it this time, and it never occurred again. However, something equally unnerving happened to her and Karin. They were both sitting in the living room when they heard "Christine" called out in a very loud voice. This was followed by, as they described it, "maniacal laughing," coming from behind the basement door. I was so happy Karin was almost completely moved into her lovely three-room apartment on the third floor.

We got busy painting and plastering her new bedroom. We tried to forget the last couple of weeks. Things were pretty quiet for a few days and we were enjoying the feeling of newness produced by all the fixing up. I kept thinking all the unusual things would just stop once no one was in the basement any longer. Upstairs seemed so bright and airy—so unfrightening and pleasant compared to downstairs. We moved all her furniture up there, and celebrated finishing all this work by having dinner at a local restaurant.

The pleasantry of the last half-week or so had also affected me and my husband. We slipped into one of our "let's-try-again" phases. At the restaurant we laughed and joked with our daughters, and everything seemed like it would just somehow work out fine. I had a sense of renewed hope and joy, and it was a very good feeling indeed.

During times like these I was always surprised when I remembered how charming and bright my husband could be. It made me recall why I married him in the first place.

We had a long and lovely respite for about six months. Karin loved her new room and I was relaxed and happy at work and at home. Christine was doing great in school and had lots of friends visiting in the afternoons. Dinner time had us all sitting around the dining room table talking and laughing about the day's events. Even when my husband and I argued, I just let it go. I really didn't want anything to disturb the quiet. Neither I, nor Karin, had experienced any suffocating dreams, and it really seemed like all of that was in the past. I did ignore the watching feelings, and continued to go to the laundromat on occasion, but I was so grateful for the break, I really didn't want to think about anything concerning our haunting.

I also knew that our "let's try again" attempt hadn't really worked. The surface of our marriage seemed better, but underneath lurked all the problems we'd always had.

We hadn't gotten along from the very inception of our marriage. We were very different people who had a hard time letting go of each other, a hard time admitting that it wasn't working out. It meant failure to both of us. A few years down the line, we would divorce—a divorce that was really quite inevitable, and one that we were both very wrong about. It did not mean failure, but freedom, for both of us. But, we hadn't reached that point quite yet.

After Karin was in her newly decorated bedroom for a few months or so, she began to experience what she termed "growling/breathing" in the middle of her back. I asked her to be a little more specific.

"Well," she said, "sometimes when I'm getting ready for bed, or listening to music, or relaxing, I start to feel a creepy sensation at the top of my back and then I hear whatever it is, growling. Then I hear what sounds like rasping breaths. Once I hear it, I feel a fear that goes right through the middle of my chest. It makes me feel really nauseous." She looked very sincere about this.

"Do you want to come back downstairs and sleep on the couch?" I offered.

She smiled. "What do you think? No, of course not! Whatever it is didn't hurt me. It just makes me feel weird. I'm sure it will go away."

I looked at her and smiled back, but I wasn't smiling inside. I didn't want to think that whatever was in the basement could be upstairs as well. She didn't know it, but by telling me what happened to her, my hopes for all of this to stop ended abruptly.

I asked her, "Karin, have you seen the Mist anywhere upstairs?"

"You know, Ma," she replied, "now that you mention it, no, I haven't. I haven't even felt like it was going to come around. I wonder what happened to it?"

Personally, I didn't know either, didn't want to know, didn't care. I was just glad it hadn't gone upstairs. Karin went off to visit a friend, Christine was looking at the TV and I just sat in the kitchen and tried to tell myself that what happened to Karin upstairs was probably nothing. It was short-lived and very subjective. I wasn't going to worry about it. I should have seen it for what it really was—a warning of things to come.

For a few nights prior to Karin's experience upstairs, my bedroom was getting uncomfortable again. The air felt thick and heavy and I had a hard time getting in a good position. I had thought maybe I was overtired or coming down with something. I didn't want to remember that the bedroom always felt this way just before a new onslaught of the suffocating dreams. The very night Karin heard the growling noises in her room, the awful dreams returned. To both of us.

When we awakened in the morning, I knew I had a tired and worried look on my face. As I cooked everyone eggs, my mind was on what a bad night I'd had. I must have experienced those dreams three or four times, each worse than the last. I was pushed into my bed, my legs and arms were stroked. I was once again terrified. It only took twenty-four hours to get to the same level of fear I had six months ago.

I was very sad. I looked toward Karin and I knew she knew. She just nodded her head and I understood she'd been subjected to a bad night herself.

As I was walking her to the door before she left for school, I asked her if she thought we suggested those dreams to ourselves.

She looked at me, half upset, half disgusted. "Mom, would you just stop! Put away your pocket Freud and stop doubting yourself and me. What we feel is real, what is happening is real. Whatever it is, it's real." She kissed me on the cheek and went down the steps, briefly looking back to acknowledge my plea to put on her scarf. I felt so scared and confused.

My husband and Christine were still eating breakfast when I got back to the kitchen.

Chris finished her eggs, got dressed, and I drove her to school. In the car she talked about her friends and her homework and looked quite happy, so I assumed nothing unusual had happened to her. I didn't want to ask, nor did I want to relate my own bad night to her. I just kissed her when she got out of the car and drove back home.

I was surprised to see my husband still there, sitting in the dining room. I hadn't noticed before, but he looked very pale.

"What's up?" I asked, "are you okay?"

He really did look ill. "Last night I had one of those, what do you call them? suffocating dreams," he said. "It was a very bad one." He'd been sleeping in the second-floor bedroom now for almost two months. "I thought they wouldn't get me up there," he continued. "I thought they just happened downstairs while I was sleeping next to you."

I gave him an indignant look.

"No, no. I didn't mean just because I was sleeping next to you. That's not what I meant. It just never happened upstairs before. And there's something else. After being woken up by that feeling of being pushed into the mattress, I sat up and tried to calm down. I looked toward the end of my bed and saw the partially formed figure of an old woman. You should have seen her. She was emaciated and I could almost see right through her. I must admit, I don't know what the hell happened last night."

I held back my intense desire to be smug. "Why didn't you come downstairs if you felt so scared?"

"Well, it wasn't that I was so scared. It was just that I couldn't figure out what was happening to me. I think if we just keep our heads, whatever it is will just go away."

I just looked at him and shook my head. "Can we sell the house now?" I asked, knowing what he'd say.

He laughed. "Don't start that again. I've got to go to work. I'm okay now."

Gee, I was so glad *he* was okay. I couldn't figure him out. I wondered what he needed to have happen in order for us to leave. I wondered why it didn't concern him that something like this was infecting our home. I went back into my bedroom after he left and tried to get a little sleep, but was very unsuccessful. The night before was too clearly etched in my mind. I went instead to Christine's room and cuddled up on her twin bed. Here I managed to get a few hours of desperately needed peace.

6 Once again, the house began to vibrate with activity. Our balls of light were back, whizzing through the rooms a few times a week. Ditto for the little, dark, scurrying shapes. I now considered the basement completely off limits and, unless I was accompanied the whole time, I routinely washed the clothes at the neighborhood laundromat. Worst of all, those damn suffocating dreams were an almost nightly event, leaving me tired and fatigued, and not at all a happy camper. I was glad, however, that they did not affect Karin's ability to get a good night's rest.

My husband never spoke of his experiences again. Whether they stopped, or he just slipped into denial, was unknown to me. He would not talk about it. Christine was faring the best. She did not seem particularly troubled by any of this, although she was frightened on occasion. Karin seemed to, at some point, consider the entities in our house to be of a protective nature, and thought we should be able to live harmoniously with them. I remained anxious to sell the house and continued to look for a way "out."

One evening, when my husband was on a business trip, the kids and I decided to have a "living room picnic," something we'd done once in a while ever since they were small children. We spread a blanket out on the living room carpet and had fun stuff for dinner, like pancakes and ice cream. This was a particularly significant and poignant "blanket dinner" because Karin had just enrolled at a college in Farmingdale, Long Island. She would now have to travel an hour to and from school, and after her first semester we would decide whether or not to get her an apartment out there. I wondered if we'd ever have this kind of silly dinner again. As we ate and laughed, I looked at my daughters' faces and felt choked-up inside. One was now in college and the other in junior high. My children were growing up so fast. I wished, for a moment, I could put my foot out and press some sort of brake, slowing down the invisible and persistent strands of time. But, snapping my mind back to the present, I was happy to enjoy their giggling and the delicious vanilla fudge ice cream.

While we were eating, Karin said, "Hey, Ma, remember when M-ow did those strange things with the carpet upstairs?"

I had almost forgotten about that. It was the strangest thing. When my husband first moved his business out, and before he relocated his bedroom up there, the second floor went mostly unused. He had removed the carpet from the front room and taken it to his new office. The only thing left on the floor was the rubber padding used as a lining for new carpeting.

While we were still sleeping together in the back bedroom on the first floor, I would sometimes, in the middle of the night, sneak into the living room to watch TV. This was as much due to his snoring as to our differences. I'd bring a blanket, lay down, snuggle into the love seat, turn on the TV and try to get some sleep.

On one of those nights, during a rather quiet spell as far as the house was concerned, I noticed M-ow behaving very strangely. The bottom of the stairs leading to the second floor were clearly visible from the love seat. I noticed M-ow sitting bolt upright, staring intently toward the upper landing. I didn't think much of this and continued to watch TV, half asleep. Then I noticed she would walk into the living room, check the couch (where Karin was sleeping), walk across the room to where I was lying down, and pause for a moment, right in front of me. If my eyes were open, she would just sit there, staring at me. When I pretended to be asleep, she'd walk across the dining room, into the back bedroom where my husband was. Then she'd walk out of that bedroom and into Christine's. It looked like she was checking on us to make sure we were all asleep. After checking on Christine, M-ow walked through the house again and stopped at the foot of the stairs.

I observed her doing this same ritual four or five times. If she saw me notice her, she stopped dead in her tracks, so I continued to pretend to be asleep.

After the fifth check, she again took her position. She sat very straight, head held upright, very regal-looking, like an Egyptian cat. After a few moments of staring like this, without moving a muscle, she would let out a soft "meow" and go upstairs. A few moments later, she'd come back down with a piece of the rubber padding in her mouth. After placing the piece on the floor, she would do her checking ritual again, and then return to her station. When a few moments had passed, she, as if responding to a signal, would let out that soft "meow," go upstairs and get another piece of padding, come down, and place it next to the other one. She appeared so odd, so robot-like. I surreptitiously watched her do this over and over again.

I tried to figure out what she was doing. It was hard to see the pieces on the floor from my vantage point on the love seat, but they seemed to be forming a shape. I waited for her to complete the checking part of her strange cycle, and, when she was upstairs, got up and investigated. Right there, on the linoleum floor at the bottom of the stairs, was a three-quarter finished circle of these small pieces of rubber padding, all spaced equally about one inch apart. She was making some sort of a design. Our *cat* was making a design.

I managed to get back to the love seat quietly, but before I did, I gently nudged Karin and asked her to wake up for a few minutes and watch what M-ow was doing. She was really half asleep when M-ow came back downstairs, but awake enough to observe what our cat was doing. When Karin realized M-ow seemed to be listening to something at the top of the stairs, and making a design, she awakened fully. We looked at each other and I just couldn't contain myself. I jumped off the love seat and woke up everyone else. The commotion caused M-ow to abort her apparently appointed task, and she sat in the corner of the dining room, looking perfectly normal.

My husband, looking at the circle of small rubber bits sleepily, said, "Look at that! I'm going back to bed."

Christine, Karin, and I slept together in the living room, not actually falling asleep until I swept up the circle and after we watched television for a while. I began to understand that, when we were at our most frightened, we used the TV as a dulling tool, embracing its tranquilizing effect.

Before actually falling asleep I kept thinking about M-ow's behavior and I couldn't figure out what the significance of it was. I wondered what would have happened it I'd let her finish her circle of rubber. Her movements that evening certainly seemed to be purposeful and directed, but by whom, or what? And why? My sleep was fitful that night, but fortunately not punctuated by a suffocating dream.

M-ow's behavior changed after that night. She seemed to become very protective of all of us, especially if we were to venture up to the second floor. As we approached the stairs she would run ahead of us and seem to check out each room first, even the bathroom. Then she would position herself at the top of the stairs and wait for us to go back down. Many nights she stayed downstairs, poised at the entrance of my bedroom, taking on the "pounce" stance, like when a cat notices some prey.

Occasionally, she'd be like that all night. I noticed that she was particularly watchful of my bedroom and not at all interested in Christine's. I also noticed that Chris' room seemed to somehow be safe.

After a few months of this behavior on M-ow's part, I began to feel inexplicably more comfortable when she was around. She'd hiss and growl at invisible threats, she would arch her back and attack unseen forces. And she never indulged in catnip! Whenever I awakened in the midst of one of those awful dreams, M-ow would be at the foot of my bed, hissing and grasping at nothing. I wished I could see what she saw and I wished she could stop it from happening. But she was trying. She became our protector after all.

By this time we actually had two cats in the house. M-ow, of course, and Vanilla, an affectionate white Persian ball of fur.

For the most part, Vanilla seemed oblivious to whatever was going on in the house, but sometimes she would seem to play with someone or something that wasn't there. A few times she'd hiss and "climb the wall" (a good three feet up) chasing whatever. Nothing in her behavior, however, actually suggested anything paranormal. It was just that in our particular situation, we couldn't help but notice that even she would at times be aware of something unseen. The only thing she had in common with M-ow was that neither of them would ever venture up to the third floor. Never. Not even with a promise of food.

One day Karin was in her new room, listening to music. She felt a cat rubbing against her back. M-ow and Vanilla were downstairs. She saw nothing, but kept feeling the unnerving sensation of a cat positioned at her back. Her friend, Maria, walked in at this time and saw a gray cat perched right on top of Karin's back. She calmly asked who the new cat was and Karin nearly freaked. She started screaming that we had no new cat. At that point, the cat disappeared, leaving them both shaken.

All these events seemed so nonsensical to us, even as we experienced them. Nothing was done in any sort of order, nothing seemed related to anything else, and none of it fit the picture of what we had seen and read about haunted houses.

It was a hodgepodge of strangeness, a mix and match of the paranormal. And we were all getting weary.

We had a small garage next to the house, at the end of the driveway. It was old and beat up, and we only used it to store things we didn't really want. One day, after a failed attempt to clear out some junk, I left our portable phone there. Karin and one of her friends, Susan, asked me if they could make a cat house out of a portion of the garage, a place to feed some strays who were hanging around our yard.

I really didn't mind, so off they went with a few tools to build their shelter. While they were in the garage they heard jumping on the roof. Looking outside, they could see nothing on the garage roof. Karin told Susan to just ignore it and came into the house to get something. When she went back to the garage she heard Susan talking to someone. She was speaking in complete sentences, followed by a pause, as if listening to a reply, and then Susan would speak again. Karin thought this very odd, and, when Susan saw her standing at the entrance to the garage, she screamed, "What are you doing there? Who have I been talking to all this time?"

They came inside and asked if anyone had been on the portable phone. No one had. Susan never ventured into our garage again.

Later that night my husband insisted Karin go into the garage again to retrieve our portable phone.

"There's nothing to be afraid of honey. Just go get the phone," he said.

She was obviously frightened to go back out there, but she went. A few minutes later she came running inside. "Mom," she blurted out. "Mom, when I bent down to pick up the phone, I could swear I heard someone say 'I love you.' They sounded very hoarse and I heard the voice next to my right ear. I really heard it, Mom."

My husband just looked at her and rolled his eyes. Karin was very angry she had been forced to go back there.

Susan knew our house was strange. She and Karin had spoken of it many times, but what happened to her in our garage was her first personal experience here. We really felt badly that she had been spooked and felt concerned that perhaps we had to be nervous about the garage, too. We had always felt pretty safe there because it was outside and completely detached from the house. But one day, feeling particularly nervy, Karin, myself, Christine, and Maria decided, in broad daylight, to do some exploring.

We looked around the garage; nothing appeared abnormal. Our junk was still junk, but we did notice an area toward the back that was about two feet wide and six feet long, located almost a foot above the concrete floor. It was completely covered with dirt. Since we'd never attempted to clear this space out before, there was so much stuff around that this protrusion was overlooked. We had to remove a garden hose, two old bikes, and a rusted shopping cart just to get it into full view.

The walls of the garage were made of cement blocks and the floor was concrete. This was the only area with dirt covering it. From its shape, and to our dismay, it looked like a coffin. We decided we needed back-up.

We enlisted the help of my brother and a male friend to help dig up this area. When they had dug out about a foot of dirt, they hit some wooden planks. These planks were so old it was hard to remove them all in one piece. As they carefully lifted them up, a stench filled the garage—a stench very similar to the one we detected in the dirt room. It was foul. Rotting. We all left the garage to get some fresh air, and when we returned, found something very unusual. Underneath those ancient planks of wood, on top of some more dirt, lay a Bible and a palm. The palm was in the shape of a cross, the kind of palm someone might get in church on Palm Sunday. The Bible was ragged and torn, but still legible. Nothing was written inside the cover. No marks were on it whatsoever. We were all suffering from an attack of major goose bumps and were now sure this was someone's burial place.

I was scared, but excited, too. I was actually hoping this might be the resting place of the seemingly troubled spirit causing so much upheaval in our house. I wondered if we should have called the police. Perhaps they would find some bones and be able to identify the poor soul. Then, I figured, we could give him or her a proper burial, and that would be the end of our nightmare. I kept saying things like this until my brother reminded me that we hadn't really found anything yet other than the Bible and palm. So the guys continued to dig.

The dirt under the Bible and palm was very hard, very difficult to dig out. They shoveled about three more feet of dirt and then they hit more cement. Solid, hard, cement. No body. No bones. Not even any clothes. Nothing. Not one bit of evidence that this was a grave, only the teaser of the Bible and palm. They shoveled the dirt back in. When it was all neatly put back, we brought the palm and Bible into the house for some further scrutiny, but they were just old items that answered nothing of our ongoing mystery.

I decided to make some coffee and as I was about to set the table, we all found ourselves staring at the Bible and palm.

My brother, Joe, said "Um . . . I'm getting a pretty strong feeling that we should put these things back where we found them. Now."

His opinion on this was very strong and we all agreed. We were feeling the same way. We felt this was the right thing to do, so once again, before they had their coffee and cake, the guys dug up a foot of dirt and we placed the items in the exact position in which they were originally found. Then we covered them up again. We pieced together the old wooden planks and placed them back on top, finishing with a cover of dirt.

It had been an exhausting and disappointing evening. It felt like the answer to our problem was almost within our grasp, and then we lost it. It felt odd, though, wishing for a grave to be located in our garage. After everyone left, and the kids went to bed, I stared out the back window and wondered if any of our neighbors had seen or heard what we were doing. If they did, they never mentioned anything to us.

I also felt sort of sad. I felt badly that we might have disturbed some sacred spot, even though we had no evidence that anything unusual or special had ever occurred there. I also felt uneasy about going into the garage again. So did my children. Whenever we needed something in there, we would literally run in, grab what we wanted, and get out.

That night we hadn't found anything, didn't actually see anything, but we felt something was there. We just didn't know what it was.

The garage event offered us many more questions than desired answers. We were getting frustrated and tired of not being able to make sense of things. We almost wished for a normal haunting—the kind where some amorphous being, all filmy and floaty, appears nightly at the same time, in the same place, always looking the same.

We could have coped with that. It would have been simple compared to what we had to go through on a daily basis.

Instead, we were forced to put up with sporadic, unpredictable, almost irritating manifestations of something.

However, manifestations or not, life in our house still went on as usual. Karin had been in college only two months and the traveling had become worse than we thought. Sometimes she'd have to leave the house at 5:30 A.M. to get to her first class, not coming home until late in the evening. This left little time for study, so my husband and I decided to get her an apartment close to the school.

As we searched for, and found, three beautiful rooms, right across the street from the college, it dawned on me that Karin wouldn't be living at home anymore. I was not at all happy with this idea, but I didn't want to be the overprotective mother I was so often accused of being. I forced myself to look pleased when we moved the furniture out of her bedroom. I watched my husband and my brother load everything into a rental van and, with Joe and Karin in the van, and me, my husband, and Christine following in our car, I began to cry.

I was happy she was getting the chance to live on her own, close to her school. I never did that when I was her age, and I wished I had. But she was moving out. I thought of some of my friends who said they couldn't wait for their kids to leave. I did not share their views. I didn't want Karin to leave.

I enjoyed her company. I enjoyed our talks. I'd miss her face in the morning and her laughter when she spoke to her friends on the phone.

I also realized in the car that day, as the miles to Karin's apartment seemed longer than I knew they were, that Karin had become my friend. My relationship with my husband had been bad for so long, and the children had witnessed so many fights with so many ugly words, that we had gravitated toward each other. We had a bond that was more than just mother and daughters—we were friends. We hugged each other when things got bad, we cuddled together when my husband's temper exploded. We shared secrets. And I cried some more.

I had never been much of a disciplinarian, never hit my kids, never cursed at them, was always aware that words said in anger could never truly be revoked or forgotten. I was proud of this, but now I could see how, perhaps, I went too far in one direction.

My husband's anger could be very frightening at times, and although he was not a hitter either, his words hurt very deeply. At these painful times, my girls and I turned toward each other for comfort, for support, but I could see how these family dynamics were more dysfunctional than I'd thought. There was so much anger on my husband's part that I had decided, although not consciously, to make everything "okay" and pleasant the rest of the time. This didn't leave much room for discipline and it fostered more of a "pal" relationship than perhaps was emotionally healthy. I knew I didn't have to hit or curse or yell in order to discipline my children, but I certainly should have kept my word when I said things like, "If you don't pick up your toys you will not be able to watch TV tonight." I almost never followed through. I talked things out with them, and they were, on the whole, very well behaved, but still, I should have been more of a mommy in that department.

Although I had discussed this pattern many times with Ron, my therapist, there was something about Karin moving out that drove these insights home to me. By not being as strong as I should have been, I was now afraid I gave them the message that they were not as strong as they should be. This made me feel very sorry, and made me promise myself that I'd do anything I could to change their perceptions. Karin going off to college, especially a college in the same state, should not have been so traumatic for me. I wasn't sure how it was for her, she didn't say much, but I hoped she found some excitement in it. She certainly looked happy.

By the time we reached her apartment, I made up my mind to embrace that moment and be truly pleased for her. We arranged her furniture and promised to visit every Wednesday evening. She would come home, if she could, on the weekends. We kissed goodbye with no tears. I was trying not to put my fears and hesitation onto her. The apartment was beautiful, she loved school, we loved her.

As we drove away, I looked at Christine. She was already missing her sister. I put my arms around her and said "Chris, this is what Karin wants to do and it's a good thing, not a bad thing. She gets to go to a school she loves, and we'll see her during the week and maybe even on weekends. This is part of her growing up and someday, you'll want to do the same thing." Chris just smiled and put her head on my lap. We drove home in silence. I was wrapped up in my thoughts about undoing the family dynamics. I wasn't sure where to start.

We kept our word. Every Wednesday night, Christine, my husband, and I went out to Long Island to have dinner with Karin. It really was cute, seeing her in her own place, making dinner. She cooked better than I thought she could. She was doing great in school. And she kept her word. Most weekends, she came home. It wasn't so bad after all. During the week, the rest of us were busy with our own lives. And busy with our uninvited guests.

I was wondering if things would be different in the house, as far as paranormal experiences were concerned, when Karin left. I remembered studying poltergeist activity in my class and, even though the events in our house didn't quite fit the description, still, I wondered. Also, I was hoping that just the change in itself might either stir things up or quiet them down. Neither happened. Things remained the same. The suffocating dreams were still occurring three or four times a week, and all the other phenomena made their usual appearances.

However, Karin reported that since her move, unless she was home for the weekend, she had no such suffocating dreams in her apartment. Not once.

For a brief moment, I wanted to move in with her! She experienced no other unusual activity in her new apartment either. Whatever we had here did not follow her. I was grateful for that.

Karin stayed in that college for a year and then, desiring to change her major to one that was not offered there, switched to a local college in downtown Brooklyn. She moved back home and, although we were very happy to have her back, now realized she was no longer a child. She moved back into the upstairs three rooms and life resumed as it had before. In my heart of hearts, though, it was incredibly wonderful to see her shining face at the breakfast table again. Shortly after she moved back, we had a long talk, including Christine, about what I felt that day in the car when she left.

I told them what I thought about the friendship thing and how I didn't want them to feel guilty about doing what they felt they had to do in their lives to make them happy.

I apologized for any overprotectiveness or clinging on my part and explained to them that I was trying to change. We had a long discussion that night and I think it was the start of a new understanding between us. I think they appreciated my candidness and I, in turn, appreciated their willingness to listen. I have great kids.

One night, shortly before Karin moved back, Christine and I were in the living room. I was sitting on the love seat, in front of the TV, and she was sprawled out on the couch. We were talking and I went to the kitchen to get a glass of soda. When I returned, we continued our conversation, I finished my drink and put the glass on the arm of the love seat. The furniture has large arms, measuring about twelve inches in length and eight or nine inches in width. I placed the glass in the middle of one of the arms. A few minutes later, in full view of myself and Christine, we both saw the glass lift off of the arm, make a few slow turns in mid-air, and finally hit the floor.

We just looked at each other. It wasn't pushed off, it didn't fall off, it wasn't near the edge—it just "lifted off." We both sighed, too tired of this sort of thing to even get scared. We didn't bother to fathom what this could mean or speculate if it would happen again. We wanted another respite and, as things worked out, this is what we gratefully got.

7 In April of 1993, my marriage finally broke up. It took me twenty-two years to get the courage to ask for a divorce. My soon-to-be ex-husband got his own apartment about a mile away from our home and we began divorce proceedings. The ending was surprisingly cordial. No screaming, no tirades—just a sadness at the end of what we both had once thought would be a lifetime love affair. This sense of sadness was closely followed by an all-encompassing, emotional sigh of relief. No more fights. No more tension. We were both free.

The house had a new atmosphere, too. It seemed somehow brighter, more airy.

Karin and Christine seemed to adjust to these new arrangements just fine. The divorce hardly caught them by surprise. I think they'd been expecting it for years, had even wanted it to happen. Christine was fourteen and Karin was twenty. They weren't small children any longer and they knew their father and I both loved them and that in no way was the divorce their fault. We made that perfectly clear to them. They saw their father once a week, out to dinner or a play, and spoke to him frequently. Things were working out much better than I'd feared.

Without all the arguments, the house seemed less "inhabited." The anger cloud was gone. The sun even seemed to shine more brightly through our dining room windows. I played my country music full blast and whistled while I got ready for work, no longer afraid that this would somehow irk my husband. My daughters seemed happier as well. It took us some time to work out a new family dynamic, but we did it with mutual cooperation and joy, and managed to go over the bumpy spots without getting badly injured. It really was a very happy time.

We'd been living in the house for ten years already, eight of which were filled with intermittent spurts of paranormal activity. We'd survived all those mystifying balls of light and muffled voices, and Karin and I endured the miserable suffocating dreams, as well as all the other events we, and Christine, grew to dread—the latest being the sound of our names whispered right in our ears. Now the house seemed so quiet, so peaceful, we began to convince ourselves that all those things were behind us. The atmosphere in the house was absolutely great. It had never felt like that before. I started to think that perhaps it was the tension of a bad marriage after all. Even after all this time, I had hopes all would be well.

The house fully cooperated with our newly found notion that everything would somehow just be fine. More than six months went by in total normalcy. We did not experience even the feelings of being watched, which had been there from the very beginning— indeed, had been there even through previous quiet periods. The suffocating dreams were gone—our nights were spent in serene sleep uninterrupted by these savage experiences. We'd had six months respite before, but not from *everything*. This felt like a significant break, an unspoken promise of continued peace.

My job in the ER was going very well. Karin was doing great in college and Christine had entered high school with lots of friends and great expectations.

At the age of forty-five, I'd even had a date or two! It was fall, the tree outside, the tree I first fell in love with, was bursting with color. We decided to have a Halloween party. Karin and Christine invited some of their friends, and I was thrilled to invite not only my friends but some of my coworkers as well. One of the guests was a supervisor of nurses at the hospital where I worked. I had known her for about three years, and in that time had never mentioned the strange goings-on in our house.

After a few enjoyable weeks of preparing for the party, the night had finally arrived. The house was cutely decorated with make-believe spider webs, and jack-o-lanterns with candles inside served as centerpieces for the tables. I felt very happy that night except for one thing. A few nights before the party, I'd had a suffocating dream. The very night before, I'd had another one, a particularly bad one. Not only was I paralyzed, as usual, but I felt my legs being pried apart, the inner area of my thighs stroked rather roughly. This had never happened before. It left me terrified and unnerved. I didn't want this to happen to me again, and I refused to let myself think about it. I pushed it to the very edge of my mind and convinced myself that all was well and that I was going to have a good time at the party.

Sadly, I knew in my gut that things were starting again. I didn't share this experience with my girls. I just wanted, this one time, this one party, for everything to be okay. I was determined to have a good time and I almost did.

Before long, on that Halloween night, all sorts of ghouls and goblins and Draculas and princesses were arriving at my front door. I'd forgotten how much fun it was to throw a party! I got thankfully lost in all the costumes and conversation and holiday atmosphere.

I was drinking a delicious Black Russian when I noticed that my supervisor had arrived somewhat late. "Lorraine! How are you?" I said, greeting her with a hug. "Did you get stuck at work?"

"Yeah, you know how it is. So, whatcha drinking?" she laughed. "Can I have one?"

"Absolutely. And that's just what I'm using—Absolut!" I quipped, as I poured her some vodka and Kahlua over ice. "Head on upstairs. That's where most of the guests are."

She handed me her coat, I gave her the drink, and she went up to the second floor while I put her coat on my bed.

By this time we had converted my ex-husband's former upstairs bedroom to my bedroom. The playroom in the back was now Christine's room and the dining room was still, well, a dining room. It was here that there was food, more drinks and music. And we were having a wonderful time.

I remember sitting in the living room downstairs, sipping my second drink and watching all my friends, and my children's friends, having fun. It was such a good feeling to have our house open to so many nice people. Since my husband's absence, I had redecorated the living room, putting up warm, brown paneling. The downstairs dining room was now painted a dark green with white trim, colors that my ex-husband had hated. He preferred pastels. The bay windows were now framed with white lacy curtains and it set off the dark green so beautifully. The back bedroom, for reasons I do not remember, was now referred to as the "cheese-box." This was the bedroom my husband and I slept in for so many years, before he started sleeping upstairs. I converted it into a sort of exercise area/den, and, next to it, what used to be Christine's room was now an extra or guest bedroom. I liked the way the house looked and I liked the way it felt. I was so happy my guests seemed to be having such a great time.

The party was well on its way. There must have been twenty-five people dancing and talking and eating, upstairs and down. But my coworker, Lorraine, seemed to be very quiet. I noticed she wasn't socializing much and I wondered if something was wrong. Perhaps she wasn't feeling well.

I walked over to her and said, "Are you okay, Lorraine? You look very pensive."

She grabbed my hand and asked me, quite casually, "Do you know your house is haunted?"

I was terribly taken aback. "Why do you say that? Have you been talking to Karin and Christine? Did you see something? Why are you saying that?" I was shaking.

"Elaine, I haven't spoken to anyone yet tonight. But I've got to tell you, I keep seeing a small woman, dressed in white, huddling under the second-floor stairwell. She looks terrified. She really is tiny. She looks like she's ready for a wedding."

My thoughts were spinning. Just a few weeks before, Karin, Chris, and my mother had been clearing out an old storage space in one of Karin's rooms. This space was located in an area behind one of the walls, almost completely hidden by wood paneling. They were so excited that day. They'd found old newspaper clippings, some from as far back as the late 1800s. They found ancient-looking tobacco boxes and a few beat-up children's toys. They also found, wrapped in newspapers from the mid-1950s, a yellowed wedding dress, size four. We found it interesting, but did not think much of it at the time. We kept it for a few days, then threw it out.

I was still lost in thought when Lorraine added, very calmly, "The little lady is not the only spirit in your house, you know. There are others and they like taking the form of little balls of light. I see them by your ceilings. And they're not the only ones. You've got quite a few here. I just thought you ought to know."

She thought I ought to know. Of course, she had no idea what my family and I had been going through. She had no idea what her comments meant to me. I toyed with the idea that she was just joking with me. After all, it *was* Halloween. I was staring at her, thinking that maybe I should open up to her, tell her what we'd been experiencing, but I was hesitant. She was my guest, yes, but she was also my supervisor at work. I had a very responsible job in the emergency room. I was afraid of what she would think of me if I admitted to her that I, too, thought my house was haunted.

"Listen, Elaine," she continued, noticing my wide-eyed silence. "This is no big deal to me. I've been experiencing this sort of stuff for years. Actually, I think I'm very sensitive to psychic phenomena and it's nothing to be afraid of. I have talked to, and seen, spirits of those who have passed on. When we moved the emergency room to its present location, I went back to the old ER and ushered many spirits to their new surroundings. I didn't want them to become confused. They had died in the old ER and I was afraid they wouldn't know where to go when we moved. Sometimes traumatic deaths cause some spirits to linger longer than they normally would."

Lorraine spoke this way without shame or embarrassment. She seemed to totally accept these things without fear or doubt. How I admired her attitude. At work, I knew her to be a wonderful, competent, compassionate nurse with a good sense of humor. In the ER we all looked up to her. She was fun to work with and someone on whom we could rely when we needed a helping hand, had questions, or if we just needed someone to talk to when the pressures of the job became too great. She certainly wasn't crazy. I continued to listen.

She went on, "You seem so scared somehow. Don't be. Seeing, hearing, feeling, or sensing things that could be categorized as paranormal is nothing to be ashamed of. Sometimes I still see my father, who passed on many years ago. He visits me at breakfast and we talk. Are you okay? You look upset."

I was ashamed of what I was thinking. I was wondering to myself if she was stranger than I'd imagined her to be. I felt hypocritical and angry at myself for judging her so harshly. I wanted to hide what was happening to us. She was so open about her experiences, so accepting of them. She reminded me of Karin. I wanted to cry, but instead, I asked her to sit with me in the dining room, where there weren't many guests, and we talked for over an hour. The rest of the party seemed to fade in the distance.

It felt so good to unload my problems on her, to know she was not unfamiliar with some of my own experiences. I told her everything, even about the suffocating dreams. She wasn't very impressed, just interested.

"I had no idea you'd understand," I said. "I wish I would have known earlier. It would have been great just knowing there was someone at work I could talk to."

She was so nonchalant about the whole thing. "There really is nothing to be afraid of Elaine. You should learn to live with the spirits you share your home with. And you'd be better off trying to get rid of your fear. Spirits are everywhere. Some people experience them and some people don't."

At that point, other guests started entering the dining room, and we both began chatting and laughing with other people. Once in a while, though, I'd look at her while she was talking to someone else and I'd still wonder if I did the right thing by confiding in her. It wasn't that I didn't trust her, it was just that the ER was a place where no one knew about my house, and now that had changed.

As grateful as I was to Lorraine, she ruined the party for me. I kept looking for the little lady. I was glad when everyone left, and then I was scared *because* everyone left. I didn't tell my daughters about our conversation until the next day. They were so happy I just didn't want to ruin their night.

Apparently, the party ruined the next few days for Lorraine as well. She called me the next day. "Elaine, I am never, and I mean *never,* coming to your house again. I brought home a friggin' light show with me! Little balls of light kept me up all night and I just know they followed me home from your house. You have a worse problem than I thought. You have to get your house 'cleaned' and you should do it soon."

She was really upset. After a few more statements, she hung up. She wasn't angry, and she kept her sense of humor about what happened, but I could tell she wasn't at all happy. I was sorry she brought home a light show, and at the same time, I was glad they went home with her. I figured she could deal with them better than I could. Then I felt guilty for feeling this. I also wasn't quite sure what she meant by having my house cleaned. She was adamant about not coming back to my house until this was done. I imagined acquiring some sort of spirit "roach motel"—they check in but they don't check out. I wondered where I could find such a cleaner.

At work, whenever I saw her, I felt uneasy. It was ER business as usual, but I knew that she knew and it made me feel uncomfortable. I was happier when it was still a secret. Since we started experiencing balls of light again, I kept wondering if they'd left her and came back to me, or if I'd gotten a new batch. It was never mentioned again, and I was hesitant to ask. However, we still remained friends, and I was glad about that. She was such a good nurse, such a funny person, that I would have hated to have her dislike me or treat me any differently because of what had happened in my house and what she apparently brought back to hers.

Our break was resoundingly over. The suffocating dreams were on the increase again. They seemed worse in my new upstairs bedroom. They lasted longer and were even more frightening than usual. Karin, when asked, said they stayed the same for her and had not increased in intensity. I was thankful for that. My upstairs bedroom was where my ex-husband had also had some frightening suffocating dreams. We were talking on the phone one day when I complained about how intense they'd recently become.

He hesitatingly told me, "Well, actually, one night, after having one of those nightmares, I heard a noise, like a loud 'thump.' I looked toward the corner of the room and saw a dark figure, very large, brownish. It had no shape and it kind of floated across the room. When it was right by my bedside, it lingered for a few moments. It seemed almost evil to me. That time, I really was scared. By the time I'd decided to get the hell out of there, it disappeared. So I put on the light and took a few deep breaths. I went to back to sleep after a half hour or so. Sorry, I forgot to tell you about that. You know, Elaine, now that I'm out of the house, I've remembered how comfortable a night's sleep can be. Why don't you sell that house and forget about all of this? Get rid of it."

He was so understanding now. He finally figured out why I'd wanted to sell the house all these years. I knew the house would be mine in the divorce settlement, and I didn't waste any time going to real estate agents. I was told over and over again that it was not a sellers' market and I was offered ridiculously low prices for our home.

I knew that now, as a single mother, and a nurse, I would simply not be able to afford another home unless I got a reasonable price for this one. I decided to wait the market out. I was beginning to feel a little desperate.

My nights were getting more and more uncomfortable. I had shifted to the daytime tour again because, now that my ex-husband wasn't living at home, I didn't want to leave my daughters home alone all during the night. I was frightened of burglars or of one of them getting sick in the middle of the night and my not being there. So, there I was again, the insomniac nurse. After only a few weeks, I managed to get on the evening tour, working 3:30 P.M. to 12 midnight—a reasonable compromise, but I still felt exhausted. My sleep was being interrupted two or three times a night, four or five nights a week, by these horrendous pressure sensations, worse and more paralyzing than before. Now they seemed to have a content that made me feel more violated than before. I was not actually molested, but the line was getting closer.

My thighs were being stroked, and I was waking up with the added feeling of fear that the next time would contain some sort of sexual assault. It was like wondering if an intruder would enter your window and rape you the next time you fell asleep. I was on edge most of the time now. I did not want to go to sleep. Karin told me that, although her dreams had not increased or changed, she felt they were somehow more urgent. She, however, managed to still not be afraid of them.

I never did see the little lady so succinctly described by Lorraine, but one evening, in an effort to avoid the feelings and suffocating dreams occurring in my new upstairs bedroom, I found myself on the couch once again, trying to get some sleep. I had a dream. In the dream, an old woman, a *very* old woman, partially skeletal, was touching my left breast. I woke up and for the first few moments, thought to myself that it was only a dream and nothing to be afraid of. However, when I was fully conscious, I noticed that my left breast was showing a hand indentation on it and I could hear the sound of the material of my pajamas being touched. I screamed loud and long. I was surprised I didn't wake up the neighborhood. My daughters came running. I was so grossed out, so frightened—nearly to the point of nausea. I had no idea what this meant. I wondered why an old lady was involved and why there seemed to be the addition of a sexual connotation. I hugged both my nearly grown-up children and cried.

I thought of going to my parents' house, but it was 3 A.M. I thought of calling my ex-husband, or my brother, but my daughters convinced me not to do this. We all decided to once again sleep together in the living room. As I watched Karin snuggle into the couch, and Christine get comfortable on the recliner, I prepared the floor with a quilt and wondered what I was going to do about all of this.

I still tried to figure it all out. I wondered what the skeletal old lady could possibly represent. I wondered what would happen next. I knew I wanted it all to just stop.

I always thought I'd be safe in the living room, on my comfy love seat, but now I was uncertain about even this small safe haven. I turned on the TV and tried to get back to sleep. But I knew. I knew things were picking up speed, and I wanted us out of all this as never before.

8 Everything came back. Once again the balls of light came floating in and out of our rooms—sometimes three or four at a time. Those small, dark, amorphous shapes decorated our baseboards most of the time. Our names were called out, sometimes quite loudly, and it almost became a joke.

We'd go around the house screaming, "What?" . . . "What did you say?" not knowing if we'd been summoned by one of us or one of "them." For myself, and for Karin, the most upsetting increased incident was the intensification of the suffocating dreams. It felt as though we were being punished for some unknown crime.

I wasn't sure we could cope with all of it again. I wanted to sell the house, even at a loss. I figured anything was better than continuing to live in this oppressive environment. I asked Karin and Christine to come to the kitchen one evening to discuss this matter.

"Okay, kids, we have got to do something about the house. I want to sell it, but I want to know what you think. I really feel we've got to get out of here."

Karin got very upset. "I don't want to move. Are you kidding? I love my rooms in the attic. Come on, Mom, can't you understand that? They're so private, so cozy. I'm not giving that up. It's the closest thing I've had to my own apartment since I went away to college last year. And what about Grandma and Grandpa? They don't want us to move away from them either."

She was so vehement about not selling the house that I turned to Christine for support, but she was crying.

"I don't want to move either, Mom. I've got so many friends here and so does Karin. I've known these friends all my life. And what about school? I don't want to leave my school either. Don't sell, Mom. Come on, don't sell."

I could understand their sentiments. I didn't want to leave my parents or my friends either. "But guys, what about all the weirdness, what about all the stuff we have to put up with in order to live here? I can't stand it anymore, can't stand not ever feeling relaxed in my own house."

Christine, her tears beginning to disappear, reminded me, "I never even had one of those dreams you and Karin talk about. Nobody bothers me at night. And, anyway, they'll all go away soon. They always do."

"That's right, Mom," Karin added. "In a few weeks, or months, it'll be quiet again. Besides, I don't lose any sleep over those suffocating dreams. I don't like them, but they don't hurt me. You get much more scared than I do about them. Actually, sometimes I don't even tell you about some of the things that happen to me just because I don't want you to get any ideas about selling the house."

I backed down. "I need to think about this, but I want you both to understand that it is a real possibility." They were not happy when they left the kitchen.

I didn't want to make them miserable by moving, but I knew I had to do something. If selling the house became my only option, I was willing to go through with it.

That night I did a lot of thinking. I wondered if I was only looking at the negative side to remaining in the house. Perhaps I was so tired of living with some unnamed, imponderable terror that I was no longer able to see past it. I, too, had reasons not to sell. I had some friends living nearby who were there when my children were born. We had memories together that went back over twenty years. We saw our children grow up together, remembered all the birthday parties, all the lunches at fast-food restaurants. Now, we were even beginning to share tales of our children's boyfriends and girlfriends. We got together on a regular basis and, even more importantly, we provided emotional support for each other.

My parents lived only a few blocks away, too. Now that they were getting older they said they felt safer knowing I was so close by. When the weather was bad, I'd call them to see if they needed anything so they wouldn't have to venture out into the rain or snow or cold. They didn't drive or own a car, so I brought them to their doctor appointments. We got together all the time for dinner, or lunch. They were extremely close to their grandchildren. I had asked them a few days ago if they'd be willing to also sell their house. I thought, perhaps, we could all go upstate somewhere, away from the city, moving "en masse," but they felt too old for such a thing, and they had friends here, too.

I was beginning to understand how involved a move would be. I also thought of my job. I loved it. It was only a three-minute drive from home. I was able to come home on my break and have dinner with my girls. This was very important to me, especially since their father was no longer living with us.

When I'd had all those arguments with my ex-husband about how I wanted to sell, I never sat down and actually thought it out. I would just get angry at him for saying "No." I decided to put this idea of selling on hold for a while longer, to Karin and Christine's delight, but I went to real estate offices just the same. I wanted to see what was available.

I had seen some lovely homes in one of the real-estate books, and happened to mention this to my ex-husband.

"Elaine," he said, almost laughing. "I know you got the house in the separation agreement, but it won't be yours to sell, legally, until we are actually divorced. Didn't you know that?"

No, I didn't. I called my lawyer and confirmed this fact. It was 1993—the divorce might not be final until 1995. So, at this point, I was barking up a nonexistent tree.

The only good thing about looking at other houses and talking and thinking things over was that I, at least, got to weigh the pros and cons. One "con" that had only recently occurred to me was that selling the house meant someone else, some other family, would be living here. I imagined them coming to check it out, their children running in and out of the rooms. Maybe they'd fall in love with the dining room or the French oak doors, as I did so many years ago. Perhaps they, too, were coming from a small apartment, or a cramped, smaller house. Maybe they had their hopes and dreams tied up in what would be their new home. Was I going to inflict this house on some unsuspecting couple? I knew if I mentioned the haunting, they'd surely not want it, but if I didn't, I didn't think I could live with myself. I wouldn't be able to snuggle comfortably in a new house knowing what they might be going through. I couldn't do that.

There I was, financially and legally trapped. Emotionally trapped by wanting to fulfill my children's wishes, my parent's wishes, and my own. And now I had the realization that I was morally and ethically trapped as well. I knew I had to find another way around this problem. I started reading up on psychic investigators. I wanted to know how houses like mine got cleaned. In the meantime, I braced myself for the latest onslaught.

I'd had such hopes for that upstairs bedroom. It was at least twice the size of the cheese-box room I'd been sleeping in on the first floor. It had beautiful blue carpeting (newly placed over the padding M-ow had found so compelling), attractive, weathered paneling on the walls, and, best of all, a balcony. The branches and leaves of that beautiful tree cascaded onto the railing. It was such a great place to have a cup of coffee, or read and relax. I loved the way the sun came streaming into the bedroom in the morning. The problem was when the sun went down and starlight could be seen through the glass doors. Starlight meant nighttime and nighttime, sometimes, meant terror.

Getting ready for bed one evening, after taking a shower, I walked back into the room and felt that nauseating sensation of a presence. I could feel it in my back, right between my shoulder blades. I saw nothing. I tried to be relaxed and calm, but it was hard. I put on the TV and did some deep breathing until the feeling passed.

This continued to happen once in a while and I did my best to ignore it. Sometimes my kids would come in and sit on the bed and we'd talk about the day's activities. I never mentioned this presence, and they never said anything about sensing it themselves. They would comment, however, on how much "things" were increasing, but they wouldn't get too specific. Ever since I threatened to sell the house, and even when I told them I couldn't, they were hesitant about making a big deal over what they were experiencing.

One night we were talking about how many vacations we'd taken when I was married to their father, and about our one big vacation since he left. We'd gone to San Francisco with my brother and drove down the Pacific Coast highway to Los Angeles. It was the best vacation ever. We talked about sleeping in motels in Monterey and Cambria and how quaint they were. Then we mentioned other vacations—Boston, Rhode Island, Washington D.C., Pennsylvania, and the many times we'd all gone to upstate New York to spend weekends at my brother's summer house in Accord.

"Mom," Karin said abruptly. "I just realized I never—not ever—had even one paranormal experience anywhere but here. Not one suffocating dream in any of those bedrooms. Just like at college."

Neither had I. I thought that was very interesting. "Christine, how about you? Anything odd anywhere else?"

"Not really. Sometimes I get a gut feeling that something is wrong, but that's it. Nothing like what goes on here."

I knew then, for sure, that whatever was in this house would not follow us anywhere else. A very comforting thought, indeed. However, this thought did not help me cope with the entities firmly ensconced in our house.

After the girls and I would finish our conversations and they'd go back to their own bedrooms, I always felt very alone. The upstairs bedroom never had that cozy feeling of the cheese-box, but I was determined to get used to it. I tried to sleep in there and read in there and enjoy my surroundings, but I'd invariably start to feel funny. I didn't always sense a presence. Most times it felt more like a slight turbulence in the room, a vibrational sensation. Initially I thought I was so uncomfortable because none of us was sleeping downstairs. I had always been afraid of getting burglarized and I didn't think I could hear a break-in from the second floor. Only a week earlier I'd had the house alarmed, not only in an attempt to quell this realistic fear, but also in an attempt to feel safer in general. But it only brought peace of mind about burglars, nothing else. I wasn't expecting any of our spirits to trip the alarm.

We even adopted an abandoned Labrador retriever (at least part Lab, anyway). He followed Karin home one day, and after advertising for two weeks to see if anyone would claim him, we fell in love with and kept this beautiful dog. He was the color of rust, with eyes that matched his coat exactly, and he had a lovely temperament. Because we already had M-ow and Vanilla, he stayed outside and had the run of the backyard. On particularly cold or rainy nights, we brought him into the basement and kept the cats on the first floor. He was very territorial and a terrific watchdog. Karin named him "Francis," after St. Francis of Assisi, and he soon recognized and responded to his new handle. Aside from all the love he gave and received from us, I figured he, too, would help ease my fears of not hearing if we were getting robbed. But, again, peace of mind about burglars was the only peace he could offer. If it weren't for the cats, I would have had him by the foot of my bed all night long.

I continued to sleep upstairs. I didn't know where else to go. Both my daughters were up there and I wanted to be close to them. The nights in that room were almost always punctuated, sometimes repeatedly, by those damn dreams. Always the same, always frightening. I feared I would never be able to just get used to this, as my supervisor/friend had suggested. I could almost see myself becoming accustomed to the light shows, or voices, even those scurrying shapes. But these dreams? No, never. I wanted relief. Once, during this time, for two whole nights, I did get that relief. I slept well and awakened refreshed and renewed. I'd almost forgotten what it was like to sleep like that. By the third night, I was meekly wondering if maybe the intensity was over and we were due for a lull in activity. I wrapped myself in my comforter, closed the lights, and fell into a pleasant sleep.

About four hours later I was awakened, paralyzed as usual. I could see my room and the stars outside overlooking the balcony. I could vaguely hear Francis barking one of his half-asleep barks. I tried to move, but of course, I couldn't. The pressure on my chest started, slowly progressing to my whole body. I began to sink into the bed, more terrified with every moment. I couldn't scream, although I tried to. Something was different. The pressure was particularly strong and very persistent. I became aware of a female presence. The awareness was not visual, but rather sensory in nature, perhaps extrasensory. It produced a feeling located somewhere beneath the fear, in the solar plexus area of my chest, the same place one would feel carsickness. All the other times this sensation let me know the presence was male and it was heavy, sad, mournful. Even in my fear states that accompanied each and every one of these suffocating episodes, I was cognizant that the one thing I did not feel emanating from the presence was anger. I never really thought I would be hurt in any way. Terrified and involuntarily held there, yes, but not physically hurt. This female presence felt *very* angry, hostile. She seemed stronger in some ways than her male counterpart and she wasn't fooling around. It felt like she wanted my attention, wanted me to understand she meant business. But what business? Whatever she was trying to communicate to me, it was clear that it was *urgent.*

After a few minutes of this horror, it let my body go. I sat up and looked at the clock. It was 5 A.M. I put on the light, shaking, crying, and scared. I had to use the bathroom, and when I was finished, I tried to go back into that bedroom but I just couldn't, not even with the lights on. I quickly grabbed my pillow and went downstairs. I didn't want to awaken my daughters, didn't want to be so afraid. I crept down the stairs. I stood in the living room and sighed. I was too afraid to sleep on the love seat after the dream where my breast was touched. I couldn't sleep in the old "cheese-box" bedroom because all the furniture was now upstairs. I felt so ludicrous and, for some reason, humiliated. I walked to the back of the apartment and laid down on the childish twin bed in what used to be Christine's old room, a room, like her present one upstairs, that had not been part of the original house. There I slept until morning.

At breakfast, as Christine was eating her eggs, she said, "Mom, Karin came into my room last night. She said she couldn't sleep and got into bed next to me. Wait 'til I tell you what happened! While she was sleeping next to me, I woke up to go to the bathroom and I saw a cloudy kind of thing on top of Karin. It looked like a puffy-shaped lady." My heart began to palpitate as she continued. "I got so scared I just flung the covers over my face and forced myself back to sleep."

"You didn't wake your sister up?" I asked, not really believing she wouldn't.

"No. I should have, right? But I didn't. She's coming downstairs now."

I was still shaking when Karin walked into the kitchen, "Good morning, honey, how are you feeling?"

"Had a hard night," she began. "I had a very uncomfortable dream. It felt like some woman was on top of me, pressing me into the bed. It was different than usual. I don't know what happened last night."

"I saw it on top of you," Christine added. "It looked like a dark cloud shaped like a lady. I woke up about five o'clock and got so scared I went back to sleep."

"I can't believe you didn't wake me up! You just let me go through that? How could you do that? I can't believe it. Thanks a lot!."

Christine felt really bad. "Okay, okay, I'm sorry. But I got so scared."

They went back and forth like this for a while and when they simmered down, I explained to them what had happened to me, and that it happened at exactly 5 A.M.

We just looked at each other, half frightened, half relieved that we at least had corroborated what took place that night. I was very thankful Karin decided to at least speak about this particularly frightening experience. I also thought it was interesting that it was the one and only time anything unusual had ever happened in Christine's upstairs bedroom. I stepped up my reading on getting the house cleaned.

We got another two-week break, another valley following a peak. I spent the entire two weeks sleeping in Christine's old room during the night. I was working up enough nerve to go to the upstairs bedroom again, and I did, with much trepidation. My kids encouraged me. They wanted me back upstairs and I, too, wanted to sleep on the same floor with them. So, with the lights and television on, I slipped under the covers and tried to get some sleep.

I was awakened at 3 A.M., not by a suffocating experience, but by a desire to go to the attic where Karin was sleeping. I felt I was being drawn there, but I didn't know why. As I got to the bottom of the stairs I heard, very distinctly, in my left ear, a male voice saying, *"You leave us alone, we'll leave you alone."*

I was fully awake at this time and trembling like a plucked guitar string. I screamed for Karin to wake up, told her what happened, and we got Christine. The three of us slunk down the stairs, looking over our backs, and slept together in the living room downstairs.

When daybreak came, I told them I'd had enough of that bedroom. I wanted all of us to move downstairs again. Karin, of course, wouldn't budge. However, Christine promised me that if anything, anything at all, ever happened to her in her new room, she'd come back downstairs. I said it was a deal.

At this point it was almost 1994. My daughters, both born in December, were twenty-one and fifteen years old, respectively. I wanted to stay upstairs with them, but they were not babies, and I couldn't sleep in that room up there for even one more night. I hired movers to bring my furniture back downstairs, back to the cheese-box.

I gave up that beautiful room, that balcony, and the good feeling of sleeping so close to my children. I looked around my old, tiny bedroom and started to cry. I felt crazy and sad at the same time. I felt restricted and imprisoned by unseen, unknown, unreasonable forces.

On the night I moved back down, my parents came over and we had a very enjoyable dinner together. They always loved seeing their grandchildren. We laughed and joked and watched a movie. This really picked me up a bit. Sometimes, the kids and I would make silent, private jokes concerning our situation, because we knew we couldn't possibly discuss it with my parents. We had tried, earlier on, and my father thought it was all ridiculous and my mother was way too frightened a person to even think something like this was possible. Her mother brought her up to be very scared of "spooks and goblins and such," and had told her awful stories that still scared her. If I had pressed the issue, I don't think she would ever have come to our house again.

As it was, with only a few, slight references to what was going on, she wouldn't stay anywhere in the house alone. But, this dinner was an especially nice one, and we had a lot of fun. It helped put us all in a good mood.

When they left, my children went up to bed, and I calmly went to my room, turned on the TV, as usual, and fell asleep. I felt comfortable and not frightened. Around 1 A.M. I was awakened by a suffocating feeling so forceful that it actually hurt. I was being pressed into the bed to such a degree that I felt I was losing my breath. I couldn't get a sense of male or female this time. The only clear sense was of anger, rage, urgency. This one lasted a long time, much more than the usual few minutes. I was so exhausted when it was over, so breathless. I lay there for a few moments, looked up at the ceiling, and understood that I would not be allowed to sleep in this room either. My mind raced. Not allowed by *whom*? I felt demoralized and beaten. Within a few minutes, a nearly hysterical fear forced me to jump out of bed. I ran into the living room, but was too frightened to go upstairs, too scared to stay downstairs alone. I felt so helpless, embarrassed, childish. I was overwhelmed. I screamed.

Christine came running down. I was crying and she didn't know what to do. When I saw her looking at me, I felt ashamed that I was so scared, but at the same time I thought to myself that most people would have a hard time with what just happened to me. Still, the shame was there. I felt like the adult who was acting like the child.

I didn't go into detail with Christine. Although she'd seen me cry from fear before, this was coming from my gut and I was surprisingly uncomfortable to have her see me this way. She stayed with me a while and then I said I was okay and sent her back up to bed. I called my brother Joe.

Joe and I have always had an exceptionally good relationship. He'd helped me get through virtually every difficult situation in my life. He even helped me find the strength to leave my marriage. He knew all about what was happening in our house and he listened with interest and curiosity and concern. He brought me books to read on the subject and had offered, many times, to spend the night. Not wanting to impose, I never accepted. But this night was different. I felt I couldn't cope anymore.

Joe lives in Manhattan, about a thirty-minute drive from Brooklyn. It was now 2 A.M. I telephoned and woke him up, and asked him to take a cab to my house. Without hesitation, without questions, he did, as I knew he would. I waited on the front steps and felt such relief when his cab drove up. I remembered, again, why I loved him so much.

Joe was as skeptical a person as I was. He tried to find reasons for what was happening. Lately, however, he began to wonder if his initial feeling of uneasiness when he first entered my basement might have more basis in fact than he previously thought. He was becoming much more open-minded about it. We both were.

That night we stayed up for a long while, talking. I told him I wasn't bothering much lately with looking for rational explanations—something was here, something I couldn't understand and couldn't deal with anymore.

He really felt sorry I'd gotten so scared. "It's going to be okay, Elaine," putting a protective arm around me. "I was reading about other houses almost like yours. Other people have gotten help, why not you? They lived through it and so can you. We'll try to think of something in the morning. Okay?"

I smiled a little and said, "Yeah, okay. I'm really tired now anyway. Where are you going to sleep? I'm going into Christine's old room in the back. Do you want to sleep in the cheese-box?"

He nodded "Yes," and I put clean sheets on the bed and wished him a good night.

I admired the fact that he had no problem sleeping in there at all, considering how frightened I was in that room just an hour or two ago. Judging by his snoring, he fell asleep quickly, and I snuggled up into that little bed and fell asleep, secure in the knowledge that my brother was but a scream away.

About 8 A.M. that morning, I woke up and heard stirrings in his room. I got up and knocked on the door. There was no response, so I opened the door a little and peeked in. I saw him lying face up in the bed, a look of bewilderment on his face.

"What's wrong, Joey?" I asked. But I already knew.

He looked at me and said, very unconvincingly, "Nothing, really. I'm okay."

"C'mon, Joey, tell me. I know something happened. Please. Don't hide it from me to protect me because that just makes me feel worse. Please tell me."

He sighed. "I think I had one of your suffocating dreams. I woke up about an hour ago feeling like I was being pushed into the bed. There was definitely something or someone in this room with me, but when I looked around, I didn't see anything. And I couldn't move—not a muscle. Weirdest thing. I couldn't speak, nearly felt like I couldn't breathe. I tried to fight it off, but it only got worse. It seemed like the more I struggled, the harder I was pushed into the mattress. I somehow decided that fighting was useless, so I took as deep a breath as I could and tried to relax my body. It was hard, though, because I must admit I was scared. When I loosened the tension, and consciously let the fear go, the pressure let up a bit. In a few moments, it was gone. But, I gotta tell you, whatever this is, it's really angry—desperately angry. It seemed enraged at something, but I don't think it was directed at me. Very strange, Elaine. If this is what you go through every night, we've got to get you some help. *Somebody* has to know what to do with this sort of thing."

Still visibly shaken, I watched him walk to the kitchen and put some water on the stove for coffee. He looked back at me and asked, "Is it okay if I stay over again tonight? I'd like to see what happens if I try videotaping this thing. I am really curious now. Can you imagine if we actually caught something on film?"

"Can you stay? Absolutely!" I replied. "I'd love it. Can you really spare the time?" I didn't want him to take time away from his photography studio in Manhattan.

"Sure I can. Things are a little slow right now, and besides, I think you need some help here."

I gave him a hug and expressed my appreciation. I was excited that he'd be there for a while, not to mention relieved. He went to his studio to pick up some video equipment and, later that night, set up a camera on top of a tripod, aimed right at the entrance of the steps going to the second floor. The same place M-ow had "drawn" her rubber circle a few years back.

That night, Joe turned the camera on and went to sleep in Christine's old room, at my request, not wishing him to experience another suffocating dream in the cheese-box. Karin and I decided to sleep in the living room, and Christine went upstairs to her own bedroom.

We kept staring at that camera, wondering what we'd find when the film was developed—and it was very exciting. So exciting, in fact, that we just couldn't fall asleep. Since I wouldn't lie down on the love seat, I wasn't all that thrilled to be sleeping on the floor anyway, so we turned on our friend, the TV. We were happily engrossed in some reruns of *Saturday Night Live* when, about two hours later, at about 1 A.M., we became aware of a milky white, shadowy something near the bottom of the stairs. We both saw it at the same time and described it to each other the same way. It lingered there for a few moments, then disappeared, leaving a feeling of a presence still there, but we were no longer able to visualize it. We were so revved up that it might show on the video, we weren't even that frightened.

When Joe let us view the video the next day, the only thing that showed up, at the exact time we'd perceived the filmy presence, was an inexplicable interference and blurring of the picture for the five minutes or so when Karin and I had seen, then felt it. No one moved the camera, no one touched the tripod, and no one fiddled with the film. This was unusual and interesting, but certainly not conclusive of anything. The rest of the video just showed the stairs, perfectly clear. Even though Joe couldn't explain the strange interference, it was not enough to show anything paranormal. We had hoped for more.

He had to go back to work that night and said he would try the video camera thing again soon, perhaps in a different location in the house. I hated to see him leave. Having him there for even those two nights helped me to regain some of my strength.

One evening, during his visit, Joe, Karin, Christine, and I were having dinner in the dining room when we were treated to a showing of the balls of light. Four or five of them whizzed just below the ceiling of both the living and dining rooms, looking like large Tinkerbells. I noticed them and so did my daughters, but we said nothing. We were so used to them, and they never produced a fear reaction, so we just continued eating. Joe, however, seemed to be aware of them this time, but we weren't sure.

He put down his dinner fork and said, "What the hell was that?"

Now we were sure.

"Light show," Christine answered calmly, not batting an eye.

Joe just looked at her in amazement. He was absolutely fascinated. He stared at them and tried to follow them into the other rooms, but they always disappeared after entering and leaving one or two rooms, so he lost sight of them. "You know, Elaine," he said. "This house just has to be investigated. What about having a 'medium' come in?"

I looked at him and made a very bad joke. "A 'medium'? Gee, why not a 'large'?"

"I'm serious, Elaine," he continued. "There are people out there who deal with this sort of thing. I used to think maybe this would all blow over once your ex-husband moved out. The house used to be so unhappy when he was here and I wondered if that contributed to all the stuff you kept talking about. But, obviously, that's not the case. How many more nights are you going to go from room to room trying to find a place to sleep?"

I knew he was right, but the idea of a medium coming in and looking into every nook and cranny of my house was not a comfortable thought for me. However, the house wasn't comfortable either. "Okay, Joey. Could you do some research on it and let me know what you find? I wouldn't even know where to look."

"Sure I will," he said, then added, laughing: "In Manhattan, the idea of a 'medium' or a 'psychic' is not as unusual as it is in Brooklyn."

I had to laugh with him because it was the truth. Manhattan is the heart of New York City, one of it's five boroughs. Brooklyn, Queens, the Bronx, and Staten Island are the other four. Although Manhattan is just a short thirty-minute drive from Brooklyn, it is like a different world. Besides the skyscrapers, the financial district, Broadway plays, night life, and museums, there is a New Age mentality there that is not as prevalent elsewhere. In "the City," which is how we refer to Manhattan, one can find information about such a wide variety of subjects that it boggles the mind.

It is not unusual to take a walk in Greenwich Village, in lower Manhattan, and pass stores that sell items and books dealing with astrology, witchcraft, healing stones, psychics, past-life regression, UFOs, ghosts, numerology, and palm reading, just to mention a few. There are also many schools teaching courses on any or all of those subjects. It would be safe to say that if you are interested in any particular subject, you'll be able to get information, somewhere, in Manhattan.

In Brooklyn, however, although there is a great variety of stores, and we have some wonderful museums, galleries, and schools, there is sometimes a hesitancy when something "new age" is mentioned. I was surprised at being able to take a class on the paranormal in Brooklyn, but in Manhattan, this would not have been considered so unique.

I was glad Joey was going to look into getting a medium or a psychic investigator, but I had to stop my mind from conjuring up images of old, scary movies and séances where people talked to the dead. I pushed those scenes out of my consciousness and tried to keep an open mind.

Once the terms "psychic investigator" and "medium" were spoken out loud in the house, things again began to intensify. The house began to have a *hum* to it, a palpable vibrational tone, and became more uncomfortable by the day. Even some of our friends began to notice. Karin's friend Susan came to the house one night when no one was at home. After ringing the doorbell and realizing no one was there, she walked back to her car. On the way, she happened to look up at the attic and saw a dark-haired young man looking out the window. She panicked and kept calling us on the phone until we arrived home. We searched the house a few times, but found nothing. Of course, later that same evening, feeling spooked, we had another "let's sleep together in the living room" night.

A day later, Karin saw a similar-looking man sitting on her bed. She said the image appeared solid for a few moments, then it grew transparent and finally disappeared. She wasn't at all frightened or threatened by him. According to Karin, "He just looked really sad. Very benign. Actually, I felt sorry for him."

The next night, perhaps not wanting to be upstairs alone, Karin asked Maria to sleep over. In the early morning hours, I heard the alarm on the door give its familiar "beep" indicating that someone was leaving the house. I got out of bed just in time to catch Maria right outside the front door. "It's 5 A.M., Maria, why are you going home so early?"

She turned toward me and I could see fear written all over her face. "I am never, ever sleeping here again. I woke up about fifteen minutes ago and couldn't get out of bed. This heavy weight, or something, was pushing me, really hard, right into the mattress. I couldn't move and I couldn't scream. When 'it' let me go, I ran out of the room without even waking Karin up."

"I'm really sorry, Maria. Was this the first time? You've slept here so many times I actually thought you'd experienced that before."

"Uh-uh. And I'm not gonna experience it again. Never again."

With that, she bolted down the block toward her own house. She was so scared and I really felt sorry for her. As I closed the door and went back inside, I looked around at our house and understood that things were only getting worse. It was now only hours between activities, and I began to get the feeling that I was being challenged to do something about the situation.

We were all becoming increasingly exhausted. I no longer had the energy to keep up the front that I was coping well. We started sleeping over my parent's house some nights, telling them we heard noises. They liked having us there, so they didn't question us too much. At home, Christine was okay once she was in her bedroom, and slept peacefully most nights. Karin was having the dreams as often, and as badly, as I was, but she again started to express another feeling about what was happening to us. More and more she believed that whatever was in the house was quite benevolent, even protective. She said it was a very strong feeling inside of her. I wondered if she, or all of us, were beginning to suffer the same syndrome that hostages experience—learning to accept, even like, even protect—their captors.

I didn't know what to do. I was not faring as well as my nearly grown-up children. There were nights on end that I slept in my clothes, lights all on, getting very little sleep. I was going to work exhausted. Sometimes I hated to leave the insanity of the ER because I knew I was coming home to yet another night of fear. I couldn't sleep upstairs, I couldn't sleep in the living room alone. I wouldn't even attempt to sleep in the cheese-box. I felt so hemmed in. I was being relegated to Christine's old room, that nine-by-ten-foot closet doing an impersonation of a bedroom. I could have gone upstairs to her new room, but by the time I'd come home from work she was usually sleeping, and I wouldn't even venture *up to* her room alone.

However, I started to learn that I *never* had a suffocating dream when I slept in that tiny oasis in the back of the house. Previously I had only used this room in an emergency, always going back to some other bedroom. I thought the respite I got in there was due to the fact that I'd already experienced a dream in some other part of the house, or we were just in a slow period. I learned this was not true. With all the activity in the house at that time, this room stayed quiet. No phenomena ever presented themselves in there. Ever. I now understood that it wasn't just that Christine was somehow immune to the suffocating dreams, it was her room.

There was a safe place right in the house, and, except for that one time when Karin slept in there, nothing had ever happened in Christine's new room upstairs either.

The only thing both rooms had in common was that they were relatively new, added on to the original building not long before we bought it. They weren't in existence in the late 1800s or even the early 1900s. I wasn't sure what this connection could mean, but I was happy that something made some sort of sense.

It took me a month or so of sleeping in that room continuously to understand this completely, and as more time went by,

I was finally able to relax and get some sleep. I remember being so excited that I had someplace to "chill" when I came home from work, someplace where I was not afraid. The more uninterrupted sleep I got, the stronger and less stressed I felt. It was so much easier to deal with all the other daily phenomena without being tortured every night. I asked Karin if she wanted to sleep there, too, and even offered to put bunk beds in so we wouldn't be too squashed, but she insisted on staying upstairs.

It felt so wonderful to be safe in that little, itty-bitty room. The stronger I felt, the clearer my mind became. I started to think I could actually do something to rid our house of these spirits once and for all.

I read some more books, even bought a video on spirits and hauntings. I reread the textbook from my class. I was getting ready to act. I was able to listen to other people's experiences of my house a little more calmly—like the time Maria and Karin were coming home from school. They happened to look up at the attic window and saw what they described as a white figure, faceless, with a round head and triangular body, looking out the window. We searched the rooms and found nothing, but something was different inside of me this time. I didn't feel so spooked, and I didn't ask my daughters to sleep in the living room that night. I was getting as unscared as my children and I considered that at least a small step forward.

Around this time I met a terrific man, an emergency medical technician named Matthew. We really hit it off. Whenever he came into the emergency room we would find some time to talk, and we talked about everything (except my house). We had a lot in common, especially the books we read, our perspectives on life, even our taste in food. In the early stages of our relationship, well before he stayed the night, Christine had a very unnerving experience.

Karin was on the third floor and I was in the kitchen downstairs, cooking dinner. Chris came out of her room on the second floor and stood at the top of the stairs leading to the first floor. I could hear her from the kitchen, talking to someone. I called out to her and then heard her racing down the stairs. She arrived in the kitchen pale and shaking.

"Mom, mom—oh, my God, you're in here! I thought I saw you sitting at the bottom of the stairs."

"Okay, okay, calm down, Chris," I said. "What did you see?"

She continued, "I saw someone sitting on the bottom of the stairs and I thought was you. From the back I could see it was someone with short, dark hair, wearing a white shirt with darker white lines running through it and grayish corduroy pants. I really thought it was you, Mom. I can't believe this."

"Was it a solid figure, or could you see through it?"

"No, it was solid. I started talking to it, asking what we were having for dinner. Then I noticed that you, or 'it' wasn't moving. So I said 'Mom, what's wrong?' and 'it' moved its head around. It was a guy and he had those old fashioned hair-cuts, like in the 1950s—swept up in the back."

"A 'duck-tail' style, like in *Grease?*" I asked.

"Yeah, yeah, just like that. And he looked really sad, like he was waiting a long time for someone. Then, very slowly, I noticed I could see through him. He went from solid to filmy, to nothing, in only a few seconds. He completely disappeared! This all happened in the time it took me to realize it wasn't you. That's when I screamed and ran downstairs."

She stayed with me in the kitchen until dinner was ready and during that time she told me she wasn't so much fright-ened by *him,* but was more scared that she'd actually seen a ghost.

That night of Christine's first apparitional sighting, we felt very uneasy toward bedtime. Even Karin was feeling a bit inse-cure. Although I indeed felt safe in my little bedroom, all the other things were still happening daily, even hourly. We were still dealing with hearing voices and seeing those shapes and being watched. Now we became afraid of seeing more ghosts. My sufficient-sleep-induced bravery was not ready for such realistic sightings. I didn't want to bother my brother again, so I called Matthew and told him that something had frightened us and asked him to come over.

I'd only known him for a few months, but I felt safe with Matthew. My daughters seemed to like him, too, and we all enjoyed his company during those times when he was invited over for dinner. That night, he arrived at our door less than five minutes after I telephoned him. I made some coffee and we all sat down to try to explain the situation to him. It wasn't easy.

He listened intently as we all took turns telling him about the house. He was incredibly interested and very protective, very much a "don't worry, I'll save you" reaction.

I wasn't at all sure he believed a word of it, but we were very happy when he decided to stay overnight. Since he'd never stayed over before, I didn't know what to suggest as far as sleeping arrangements went. We finally decided that Karin and Christine would sleep in the living room and Matthew and I slept on the twin bed in what was now *my* room. Even with him by my side, I was not going to sleep in the cheese-box. He had a hard time understanding that I would not go near that queen-sized bed just a few feet away in the other room, but I wouldn't budge, so we tried to get as comfortable as possible on that tiny bed, both of us fully clothed. As awkward as all this seemed, I found myself drifting off to sleep with this most patient man at my side.

About 3 A.M. I awakened to see Matthew really having a tough time, pulling at the sheets and trying to turn around. Poor guy, he was still awake.

"Could we please just go inside? This bed is beginning to hurt and it's way too small for both of us. We can keep the light on if you like, even the TV. Come on, what do you say?"

I really didn't want to go in there, but I felt sorry for him. He'd run over to our house in the middle of the night, listened to our stories and now he was being deprived of a night's sleep. I hesitatingly gave in. It really was much more comfortable for both of us on that bigger bed, and I made him keep his promise to keep the lights and TV on. Before long I again drifted off to sleep.

I woke up in the early dawn hours, somewhere around 6 A.M. At first I was startled to find someone in bed next to me, but then I quickly remembered about the previous night. When I glanced over at Matthew, he was lying there, staring up at the ceiling, looking rather puzzled.

"What's wrong?" I asked.

He began, "You know, Elaine, last night, when I heard you guys talking about everything, I wasn't scared or anything, just curious. I was even wondering if anything would occur while I was here. When you first fell asleep, in that tiny room, I stayed up and listened for a while, and heard some popping and tapping noises. I attributed this to this house being so old. I began to get really restless in there, not knowing if I was anticipating something happening, or I was just uncomfortable in such a small bed. Anyway, after I convinced you to come in here, and even though you fell asleep pretty quickly, I felt disturbed in here. I tossed and turned and just couldn't relax. I tried to take my mind off how I was feeling by watching a little television. By the time I nodded out, the sun was coming up. It couldn't have been more than an hour or so ago."

I listened quietly as he continued.

"The next thing I knew, I was having a dream. In it, I was trying to open the door to that little safe bedroom. Although the door was slightly ajar, it was extremely hard to open. I pushed harder and harder. I felt a tremendous resistance, like a very heavy weight was behind the door. I pushed even harder, using all my strength. I finally began to move the door, and when it was opened, I looked into the room. I saw a flash of a picture of a skeletal man lying on a dirt ground, with his head turned toward the side. The man had strands of gray hair combed to the side, over his skull. He was wearing very old clothes that were ripped and rotting away from age."

I shuddered at his description of the dream and the skeleton.

He added, "I woke up to the feeling of having a very heavy weight on my body. It took all the energy I had to try to turn onto my left side. I felt exhausted, like I'd been struggling with something that I could not see. Finally, I became more alert and that was just a few minutes ago."

He looked very tired, and a little upset. I asked him if he thought he'd had a suffocating dream, but the night before I hadn't really gone into the description that much.

"Maybe," he said. "But for me, that dream, even the pressured waking state, was more like a message. I felt there was an answer here to some of the questions about the activity in your house. I think the man in the dream was trying to tell me something and I felt that he needed help."

I just stared at him. For some reason, at that moment, his conclusion made sense to me. My daughters also felt they needed help and, hearing Matthew tell about his dream, for the first time, I felt some compassion instead of fear. When we hugged that morning, after talking and having coffee, I felt so grateful that this new man in my life did not think we were strange and was not frightened by our house. He told me he had always been interested in the afterlife, in spirits, and he wished we had discussed the house earlier in our relationship. I explained to him that I was reluctant to bring it up because I was afraid he would think I was crazy.

"You're not crazy, Elaine," he said softly. "You just have a problem that has to be dealt with."

After that night, Matthew sort of melted into our lives and stayed over more and more. He experienced all the phenomena as well. Once he even said he took a ball of light back to his apartment, just like my supervisor said she had a year or so earlier. Matthew worked evenings and overtime as well, so there were many, many nights he couldn't stay with us. I felt so much better when he was there. So protected. Even though the suffocating dreams had stopped for me, Karin was still having them, and all three of us were bothered all night long with the noises and lights and voices. We regularly slept fully dressed, lights and TV on, and had friends over if we could manage to get them to stay.

The friends never came back—the lights on didn't help— and the clothes were terribly uncomfortable to sleep in. Having company over, having Matthew there, made things feel better, safer, but only for a little while. We needed a more permanent solution. I called my brother and asked him to step up his efforts to find us a psychic investigator, or a medium, or anyone who could help us. I was completely ready to deal with this head-on.

As if on cue, the spirits responded loud and clear.

9   The phone call to my brother seemed to prompt the increase of phenomena already known to us and herald the appearance of some brand-new ones as well. Suddenly we'd hear breathing—heavy, annoying breathing, sometimes right in our ears. It sounded like the inhaling and exhaling of someone who was excited, nearly breathless. We all experienced this and found it not so much scary as bothersome. We'd reached a point, especially me, where we no longer doubted that all of our experiences were, indeed, coming from outside of ourselves. It made it easier to deal with in some ways. We felt less responsible, less crazy, less abnormal. I think my daughters were quite relieved to have me join them in the knowledge and acceptance of the fact, not the "maybe" or "what if," but the fact that our house was haunted, and that whatever, or whomever, was here needed help. It's hard to say when this more compassionate way of thinking became solidified in my mind. I think my children had always been way ahead of me and I followed what they seemed to already know.

It was an evolutionary process of sorts, and it helped to alleviate many of the fear states we found ourselves in. However, we were still capable of becoming startled, or downright frightened, although it was different. There was a calmness to the fear, an understanding that what we were experiencing were cries for help, not efforts to torture us.

A rather embarrassing thing that presented itself to us at that time was the smell and sound of flatulence coming from nowhere. We could all see the humor in this manifestation, but could make no sense whatsoever as to its meaning. It was so peculiar.

I had never thought of "passing wind" as something to be ashamed of, and Karin and Christine didn't think so either. We

119

had no trouble laughing out loud when one of us let go. However, these sounds were not coming from us. We'd be sitting down, watching TV or reading, when we would hear, quite loudly, the familiar "pblllt," followed by an absolutely noxious smell. The odor reminded us of burning sulfur. It was just awful—foul, disgusting, putrid. It wasn't like us not to admit guilt, so we looked at the cats. We realized it would take a mighty big feline to make such sounds, and such smells, and we were sure it was coming from somewhere or someone else. We heard these nerve gas offenses when we were alone and when we were together.

I was in the dining room one day, just reading and listening to music. Someone broke wind right near my face. As my nose crinkled up in response to the thick, offensive odor, I had to laugh. If the spirits were doing this, I wondered what they were trying to communicate. I thought they must either have some sort of sense of humor, or they were just trying to get my attention, or maybe they were just rude.

When we had company over and this happened, it was very embarrassing. My daughters and I would just look at each other and try to contain our laughter. We wondered how our guests might react if they knew the farts were apparently coming from "beyond"! We used to just ignore it and continue on with whatever conversation was taking place. Our guests did the same, but we always wondered what they might have thought.

We also started hearing giggling sounds, like small, excited children anticipating a fun event. We heard this upstairs, downstairs, and in every room, except, of course, for Christine's. We also became aware of newly recognized "shoosh" sounds, the kind of thing someone would hear when they were being asked to keep quiet. Sometimes these "shoosh" sounds would occur all night long. Anyone visiting our home at that time commented on these sounds as well. We used to cover it by telling them it was coming from some neighborhood children. We were fascinated that they mentioned it at all, almost pleased that they heard what we were hearing.

We also got the feeling that somehow the spirits knew we were working on a solution to whatever problem they were having. There was a palpable feeling of excitement in the air—a sense of something to come.

We had always had a problem with an odor in the dining room on the first floor. The odor emanated from the bottom of a steam pipe leading to the basement. It smelled like something dead, and it alternated with the smell of freshly cut roses. This permeated the house most of the time now—none of us knowing which odor would dominate for the day. We tried air fresheners and candles, but this smell would end up dominating anything we tried. Mixing with the flatulence problem, it was an interesting scenario indeed.

The not-so-threatening balls of light changed in the sense that, although they were still a daily occurrence, sometimes they would sort of clump together and form one super-bright light. This light would fill up a room for only a few moments at a time and then it would leave. It was as illuminating as if the sun, for a few moments, had decided to focus its energy on one of our rooms. It always left us astonished. It was just *so* bright. If they weren't doing this "super-bright" thing, then they were taking the form of little flash pops, similar to camera flashes, all over the house. *Pop . . . pop . . . pop . . .* all day and all night long.

We were so miserable. These new phenomena were not very threatening and they had no connotation to them whatsoever of anger or injury or danger. We were just tired. We wanted to get this over with.

It was now the fall of 1994. Things had been increasing for nearly a year, with a sporadic vacation now and then. The phone call to my brother about having the house investigated occurred in the summer. We were two or three months into the latest cycle of new phenomena. My brother called and asked if he could bring over his new girlfriend, Maura. Joe had told me she was "psychic," and I was interested to see if she would sense anything unusual about our house.

Maura and Joe were due to arrive at our house one evening. I was very anxious and happy to meet Maura, happy to know she was someone very special to my brother. I was also thrilled that my newfound love, Matthew, was included in that special dinner.

When she arrived, we greeted each other and I introduced her to Matthew, Karin, and Christine. She was all smiles, as was her nature, and we all sat down at the dining room table to begin a friendly conversation about nothing in particular.

Within a few moments, her radiant smile quickly changed to a look of bewilderment. I noticed that she grew quiet, but she tried to continue with the conversation at hand and the excitement of meeting her boyfriend's family for the first time.

She suddenly stood up in front of all of us, which I thought took a great deal of courage, and said, "Look, guys, I'm sorry but I seem to be having a hard time here. I'm feeling a sort of 'heavy' sensation right on my chest and, for some reason, I feel drawn to your basement."

She looked genuinely puzzled by her feelings and I didn't quite know what to do for her.

I admired her honesty, her unassuming truthfulness, and I knew at that moment that I liked who she was.

"Maura," I asked, "is there anything we can do? What exactly are you feeling?"

She continued,"Well, actually, I think there's a 'vortex' in your living room and it leads all the way down to the basement."

"What's a 'vortex'? What does that mean?" I asked.

"A vortex is like an opening of sorts, a place where spirits can enter, or leave. A place that has to be closed if you don't want any more problems. Have you been having some sort of psychic phenomena here? I'd really like to see what's in your basement, but there's no way I'm going down there by myself."

I was so relieved that she had some level of fear in her. I had previously thought that anyone who was psychic was just automatically free of any hesitation when it came to phenomena like we'd been experiencing. Her unwillingness to just explore the basement by herself endeared her to me. I felt a connection to her. I was spooked and fascinated at the same time.

"That basement is really 'calling' to me, Elaine. Can someone come down there with me?"

I looked toward everyone at the table and got their silent, enthusiastic agreement, and then turned to Maura and said, "We'll all go with you."

With that statement, we all stood up and arranged ourselves around her, walking slowly toward the basement stairs. We continued encircling her all the way down to the basement even though we had some difficulty fitting our entwined bodies in the stairwell. It was a clumsy, but very effective, show of support.

When we got to the bottom of the stairs, Maura left the temporary security of our circle and walked to the middle of the laundry area, right near the dirt room. She spoke softly as she pointed to the dirt room and said, "This house needs to be cleansed as soon as possible. There is something very wrong in that area. I'm not sure what the problem is, but it requires immediate attention."

I felt chills going up my spine as I told her, "Maura, Joe is trying to get someone to come in and help us out. He's been asking about mediums and psychic investigators."

"Well," she replied, turning to my brother. "Joe, you need to act soon, very soon. I sense there are some souls here that are seeking relief and they are very, very uncomfortable. That vortex in the living room comes clear down to here. It's like an area of energy that's opened to the spirit world and it invites, and retains, spiritual energy. Spirits can either go through the vortex and remain here, Earthbound, confused, not really knowing they're dead, or they can escape through this energy field and go to 'the light.' In the light they will find peace. They need help and they need it now." Maura seemed so sincere, so kindhearted as she spoke these words.

After a few moments of quiet, Joe very seriously replied, "I'm really working on it. Even in New York City it's hard to find a reputable person. I should have someone soon."

"I know," Maura said. "You just need to understand that the matter is very urgent. These souls are in pain. They need help. House-cleaning is not my forte or I would attempt to do it myself. Can we go upstairs now? I'm feeling really uncomfortable down here."

With that, we all went back upstairs and back to our dinner. As the conversation returned to more normal topics, I found my mind wandering. I wondered about what had just happened. I was surprised that I found myself not even doubting for a moment what Maura had said. It seemed to ring true for me, as if she had managed to put into words what I was unable to express. Maura helped me make a more narrow turn on the corner so blatantly in front of me, and her insights seemed quite plausible to me.

I watched Maura during the rest of the dinner. She seemed to be so sweet-natured, sincere, and very rational, not the type of person given to unreasonable conclusions or irrational thought. I took her counsel seriously and told my brother that if he didn't get someone soon, I'd do the looking myself.

Joe promised me he was doing his best to find the right person. He said it would only be a matter of days until he weeded out some people he was not comfortable with, some people he wasn't sure were legitimate. I trusted him and bided my time waiting for his call.

During my wait, one afternoon I invited a few members of my family and some friends over to the house for dinner. As long as they weren't being asked to stay overnight they seemed perfectly happy to come over for a little food and conversation.

As usual, they were unaware of the balls of light or the various extraneous noises. The only thing they remarked upon was the foul odor alternating with the smell of roses coming from the dining room. My daughters and I couldn't help but laugh at all the silent accusations made that evening. Everyone blamed everyone else for passing wind, or wearing too much perfume.

During dinner, I left my company to go to the back bedroom, the cheese-box, to get my slippers. When I put on the light and entered the room, I found the bottom drawer of my dresser, located at the foot of the bed, opened up. All my underwear was scattered around the bed. No one had been in there. We were all home, all night, sitting around the dining room table. It looked so eerie—all my lingerie, my bras and panties, spread out along the foot of the bed. I choked back a scream and went back inside after closing the door and not picking anything up. I waited for the company to leave, but asked Joe to stay. After everyone else was gone, I showed him and my daughters what had happened in the bedroom.

I was very upset. "What does this mean, Joey? What? Why my underwear?"

Joe surveyed the scene. The bed in this room took up a great deal of space, so much so that the drawers of the dresser could not be completely opened because they hit the frame at the foot of the bed. Emptying the whole drawer required a considerable effort, not to mention opposable thumbs. The cats couldn't have done this.

Joe turned to me, "Elaine, I have no idea what's going on here. Don't know what is trying to be communicated, what this all means. I swear I'll have someone to help you within a week or two. Just a little more patience, okay?"

I was really reaching my breaking point. There was an element of violation in the emptying of my dresser drawers, in seeing all my personal items strewn about the room. This happened three times in only one week. One time we discovered it upon arriving home after being out the whole day. No one had been there. Nothing else was disturbed, only the one drawer in that bedroom containing my intimate apparel.

Christmas, 1994, seemed to come rather quickly. Karin and I got busy doing our decorating, both of us being Christmas fanatics. We strung lights outside our windows and outlined the porch area and shrubs in our garden. We put up a beautiful tree in the living room and had our annual tree trimming, inviting my parents over to participate. We were always really corny about this. We played Christmas carols, served eggnog, and had *It's A Wonderful Life* playing on the VCR. We enjoyed ourselves thoroughly and, just for that one night, gave no thought whatsoever to any phenomena, psychic investigators, mediums, or anything else. My parents, Karin, Christine, and I joyfully immersed ourselves in the holiday festivities.

During one of the nights of that Christmas season, Christine and I were downstairs on the first floor, playing a game called "Simon." Simon consists of a round object with four different colored, lighted areas on top. The object of the game is to play back, in sequence, the musical sounds emanating from each of these lights.

If a mistake was made, Simon made a very distinct "boink" sound. Then the sequence began all over again. We all found this game very challenging, distracting, and enjoyable, and sometimes we played it just to get our minds off the activity going on in our house.

While Chris and I were playing, Karin was upstairs on the third floor, listening to music. We heard a scream, which was very unusual for Karin, and she came running downstairs. She was white as a sheet.

I jumped up and ran to meet her. "Honey, honey, what's wrong? What happened?"

"I can't believe it. I just can't believe it." She was nearly breathless.

"I was just listening to music, kneeling down facing the picture window in my bedroom. Suddenly, I had such an urge to turn around. You're not gonna believe me."

Karin was so upset she was shaking. I held her shoulders and looked her straight in the eye. "I'll believe you. I swear. Just tell me what happened. Take a nice, long, deep breath and tell me what happened!"

"Okay," she continued. "Okay. When I turned around, something came flying at me. For a split second, I saw a flash of gold. It was aimed right at my head. I didn't know what to think, so I automatically put my hand up to my cheek. Whatever it was hit my hand and then . . . Mom. . . . and then, it *pulled back*. I took my hand away and looked at this thing. It resumed its original course and flew at me again, hitting my cheek. It pulled back again and *hovered* there, right in front of me. I gave it a hard slap and it flew behind the radiator in my room, the one underneath the window. Then I ran downstairs."

She was nearly hysterical. I don't think I'd ever seen Karin that shaken up. We all hugged and sat together in the living room and waited for her to catch her breath. I asked her what she thought the object was, but she wasn't sure. She was sure, however, that it was now behind the radiator.

We didn't want to, but we decided to go upstairs and see what was going on. We marched up there, walking so close to each other I'm sure we must have appeared soldered together. We got to her bedroom and immediately looked behind the radiator. The only thing there was a hair clip, one of those large, oval ones used to hold back a great deal of hair. It was red velvet on the outside and gold on the inside, about four inches long and one inch wide.

As we retrieved the clip, Karin identified it as the object that had accosted her. As I watched her touch the clip, I could see the puzzled look on her face. She kept looking around the room as if to find some clue, some explanation. I knew that in order for Karin to have experienced what she said she did, this clip had to fly vertically and upright—the gold inside flashing at her. More importantly, it had to have been held by something or someone in order to achieve the trajectory she described. It attacked and withdrew, attacked and withdrew—never once showing its velvet side. Karin was even sporting a visible abrasion on her cheek. We were very taken aback by this new happening, and wanted to get downstairs as soon as possible.

Karin threw the clip on her bed and we all hugged and walked, in unison, down the attic stairs, to the top of the second-floor staircase. When we got to this landing, I heard "Simon" play a tune. I honestly thought the spirits were playing the game. I started to shake and, I swear, according to Karin and Christine, the hair on my head, although rather short at the time, stood straight up. I felt like some character in a B movie. In my terrified state, I'd forgotten that when

"Simon" is left on and unattended for a while, it plays a tune to let you know you didn't shut it off. We laughed about this later, but we knew the stress of the whole situation had gone way too far. We were camping out at my parents' house or sleeping in the living room, on the same blanket, lights and clothes on, all the time. We couldn't live like this much longer.

We wanted the cavalry to arrive, soon. Joe's "cavalry" came a few weeks later in the form of a medium, and a well-known ghost hunter. I was very impressed when I called him and he told me who it was.

"I got Dr. Hans Holzer, Elaine. After all this time, asking so many people, all I had to do was mention it to a friend of mine and, boom, she knows Hans. I had no idea, hadn't heard that name in a while. Can you believe it?"

"You're kidding, right? Hans Holzer. The same guy who used to have a TV show? The one I remember when I was younger? He's willing to come to my house? How much? When? Did you actually talk to him? What did he say?" I was so excited.

"Well," replied Joey. "I wouldn't worry about the price because Hans is willing to forego his fee because of our mutual friendship. The medium, Marisa Anderson, isn't charging much either. I think he said something like $250.00 for the whole-day visit. Is that okay?"

"I guess so. $250.00? Is that the going rate? I think that's doable. When are they coming? Do I have to prepare anything special for them? I'm not sure what to do now."

"Hans said he'd let me know the exact date sometime next week. Calm down, okay? Help is on the way and I think we've got some good people here. I trust my friend's judgment. It's going to be just fine. Look at it this way—after all these years, you're finally doing something about this. And soon."

I hung up the phone feeling such a wonderful sense of relief. Two people were coming to our house who knew all about this stuff. They were going to help us and maybe, just maybe, we'd be able to live in a house uninhabited by spirits. I'd be able to explain what was happening to them without fear of being ridiculed. I was sure they'd heard it all before. I still had my doubts about the medium and even about Dr. Holzer. I hadn't followed his career during all these years. I only knew what I'd remembered about him and that wasn't much. I vaguely recalled his television show dealing with the paranormal, but I wasn't familiar with most of the books he'd written.

I had some suspicions about the whole area of psychic investigation and I wasn't willing to just blindly trust anyone. I decided to reserve judgment until I'd met them because at least then I'd have more information on which to base my impressions.

All I knew was that help was on the way. It made the next few weeks much more bearable.

10

It was mid-January, 1995. Dr. Holzer and the medium, Marisa Anderson, were due to arrive at our house February 2. The activity remained at the highest level we had ever known, and it had been this way since these arrangements were first made. We were very uncomfortable and stayed out of the house as much as possible, but we began to imagine a light at the end of this very long tunnel. The thought of this whole episode coming to an end brought with it a sense of empowerment, as if there might be some control over it after all. Although my daughters never felt like victims, for many years I had. I was slowly drifting away from this perception of the situation and could feel the stirrings of compassion for whatever, or whomever, had been causing such a disturbance in our home.

We had no idea how this investigation would be conducted. We envisioned them bringing in all sorts of equipment like infrared lights and sensors and microphones. We hoped the medium could somehow communicate with the spirits and perhaps she could tell us what we needed to do to both help them, and help ourselves be free of them. I wasn't sure when this feeling of empathy for our inhabitants developed, but I know it was a very slow, almost imperceptible, process. After many conversations with Karin and Christine, I began to see it more through their eyes. They had never been as frightened as I was, and I think part of the reason was because a large chunk of their childhood had been spent cohabiting with our ghosts. I brought all of my prejudices, cultural taboos, and learned fears to the situation, whereas they were able to open their innocent hearts and look upon our spirits as just some sort of beings in need of assistance.

Of course, they did get scared at times, and lately, so much so, that we rarely slept at home anymore. Whenever we were there, our ghosts' behavior was just so insistent. Banging, breathing, lots of balls of light, all the time. Once I even screamed at them, at the top of my lungs, "Okay, okay, we hear you. Help is on the way. Just stop. Just stop it." It did no good at all, except it made me feel better to let off some steam!

We had about three weeks to go before psychic ground-zero and we wondered if there was anything else to do besides wait. My daughters and I decided to go down to the Hall of Records and look into the origins of our house. We knew it was old, but were very surprised to find out that it was, indeed, over 125 years old. In that time, according to the records, and except for the previous owner (the person from whom we purchased the house), it had changed hands approximately every six to nine months. We were amazed at the list of buyers and sellers and thought it most peculiar. Of course our first thought was that they were all frightened away, but we had no way of knowing this for certain. It was very interesting. Our poking around the Hall of Records inspired us to poke around other places as well.

I decided to call the middle-aged couple from whom we originally bought the house. They were now living in Florida. We had their last name, so they weren't hard to find. My heart was palpitating as I waited for someone to pick up the phone. After a few rings, a female voice on the other end said a simple "Hello?"

I quickly replied, "Hi. My name is Elaine, perhaps you remember me. I bought your old house in Brooklyn. The mortgage we owed you was paid off a few years ago."

She hesitated, "Oh, yes, I remember. Why are you calling? Is there a problem?"

"Well, actually," I continued, after taking a long, deep breath, "I was wondering if you or your husband or anyone in your family ever experienced anything strange while you were living here."

There was a very long, thickly quiet silence on the other end.

Her response was very terse, almost angry, "I have no idea what you're talking about. Nothing, absolutely nothing strange, ever happened while we were living there!" This statement was followed by a rather loud, and abrupt, hang-up.

That had not gone quite as I'd anticipated. I thought that, aside from being angry, she sounded a little nervous and defensive. She didn't give me a chance to explain anything, and she denied everything before she understood what I was saying. Or did she understand very well? I couldn't tell. I thought maybe I was reading too much into her response. Perhaps she was just nervous because she thought we might sue her if we found out the house was haunted. Or, then again, she might have thought I called to complain about termites or something else she considered a liability. At any rate, this call did nothing to further our exploration of our house.

As I thought of ways to get some more information about our house's roots, I wondered why I hadn't done that before. Part of me wanted to be able to confirm or deny any information the psychic investigators might relate, but also, I was no longer afraid to stir up the pot, afraid of doing something that would cause the spirits to increase their activity. Now, with the psychic investigators coming in a little less than three weeks, I figured the pot was as stirred as it was going to get.

I remembered that one of our neighbors had been friends with the old man. I had seen them talking together frequently when we first visited the house. So, one day when I saw him in his garden, after the usual "hellos," brought up the subject of noises. I chose "noises" because it seemed a lot more benign than coming right out and asking him if he knew our house was haunted.

"Hey, John," I asked, smiling as if his response was not particularly important to me. "Did that elderly man who used to live in my house ever complain to you about hearing noises?"

We'd never shared more than a few words together in the last twelve years. John was very quiet. I started to perspire.

He looked up from his tomato plants and said, "What do you mean, noises?"

"Well, you know, noises, bumps-in-the-night, that sort of stuff."

Very sarcastically, and with a teasing laugh, he responded, "Whattsa matter, you got ghosts? I hope you don't believe in that crap. I never heard nothin'."

I was so embarrassed. I just laughed and changed the subject. That was a very hard conversation for me, but it wasn't excruciating. It wasn't *that* bad. I decided to talk to some other neighbors. I sort of sneaked the subject into our conversations. No one really picked up on it until I talked to another of the neighbors who lived very close by.

In retrospect, I should have talked to him first. Tony was one of the most friendly people on the block and we always had a "good neighbor" relationship. I broached the subject one day while we were throwing out our respective trash.

"Hey, Tony, how're you doin'? How's your wife?"

"Doing good, thanks, and you? Haven't seen you for a while," he said as he continued to try to stuff some overloaded garbage bags into a trash can.

"Uh, Tony, uh, I was wondering if the old neighbors ever told you about any strange noises they were hearing. Sometimes we hear weird sounds in the house."

Without looking up, he replied, "Strange noises? Is that all? I'm surprised that's your only complaint."

All I thought was that I'd finally hit pay dirt.

Tony wiped his hands and walked over to the front of my house and, without any prodding, began describing what had happened to him in our house when he was a teenager.

"You know, I used to babysit for those people who moved to Florida. More than once I heard footsteps up and down the stairs leading to your second floor. I used to peek outside to see if anyone was there, but there never was. Sometimes I'd even hear what sounded like some people talking, but I could never understand a word they said and I never saw who it was. The last time I babysat, and I made sure it *was* the last time, I just couldn't shake a feeling like someone was watching me. It was so intense that I nearly took the kids to my mom's house. Then those damn footsteps kept going up and down the stairs, up and down, and they got really loud. When the parents came home, I bolted out of that door and never went back. I'm telling you, that was nearly thirty-five years ago, and I still remember being terrified. How come you never mentioned anything before? I didn't want to say anything to frighten you off, and when you didn't, I just figured nothing happened there anymore."

"Nothing happened? Are you kidding. This house has been driving us crazy for years! Did you ever see anything, I mean actually see anything?"

He continued, "No, not really. I mean, I never saw a ghost, if that's what you mean. But, you know, the old couple's only son, Stephen, got married while he was still living in your house. He and his new wife, I think her name was Charlotte, lived on the third floor. This was before the other people, the ones I used to babysit for, moved in. Not long after the son was married, his wife suffered a heart attack and fell, hitting her head on a night stand near their bed. They said she died of an aneurysm caused by the fall. And she died right in that room."

He pointed up to my daughter Karin's bedroom window.

The chills rode up and down my spine as he continued. "The one thing I'll never forget about her was that she was so small, so petite. I remember seeing her on her wedding day, standing on your front steps. I must have been thirteen years old at the time and I couldn't take my eyes off her. She had the tiniest waistline I'd ever seen and she looked like a little porcelain doll."

"Tony," I was so excited I screamed. "I can't believe what you're telling me. My friend saw a small little lady hiding under our stairs one night. And we found a wedding dress hidden in the attic, it must have only been a size four." I lowered my voice down when I'd heard how loud it actually came out. "This is incredible. It could be just a coincidence, but I don't know. Anything else you remember?"

"Now you're giving me goose bumps," he replied, "but there is just one more thing. The son died shortly after his wife. They said he had cardiac problems."

"That's so sad, Tony."

We left our conversation on that note because he had to leave for work. I thanked him for being so honest with me, and as I watched him drive off to work, my mind wandered to what sadness our house must have held. By the time I closed the outside door and was walking past the living room, I got the chills again. I wondered if that was the man Christine saw sitting on the stairs, looking so forlorn?

His death would have occurred in the 1950s. The duck-tail haircut and the clothes Christine described him as wearing were appropriate for that time period. The thought connecting the apparition with this man produced tears in my eyes. My mind took off, wondering if his spirit might be searching endlessly for his young wife. I kept imagining this young couple, newly married, living upstairs from the husband's parents. The heartache the son must have endured, as did his parents after he, too, passed on. I remembered the old woman's sad eyes—she'd lost her only son. She would have no grandchildren. Only memories of what was and what could have been.

I saw her eyes a hundred times that day. If, indeed, these two spirits were in our house, somehow unsettled by their trauma, by their tragedy, then I had a responsibility to help them. I put a great deal of hope in our upcoming visitors. I wanted this young couple to be at peace.

Karin, Christine, and I were so excited by this new information we went to the Hall of Records a second time, looking for bits of information that could help further explain things. This house had been moved from its original location, around the corner, to where it is now. The entirety of the house was put on a trailer and pulled into the vacant lot that was now its permanent address.

Brooklyn is divided into neighborhoods, or sections, all with different names. Our house is located in the Gravesend section, not far from the waters of Sheepshead Bay. As

Sheepshead Bay is so named because it is shaped like the head of a sheep, I wondered where Gravesend got its rather solemn sounding name.

Apparently it was originally named by someone referred to as Lady Moody, its founder. She remains buried in the Gravesend Cemetery located only a few blocks from our house. There is a minor mention in the archives of an old Native American trail winding through this area, eventually leading to a gravesite, but it is unclear if this refers to the Gravesend Cemetery. It seems that long after the Native Americans left, or were forced out, in the late 1800s, this area became known as "Dutch Town." Most of those living here were of German or Dutch ancestry. It was a poor village at best.

Following the "Dutch town" settlement, farmers moved in, and later it became occupied by well-to-do settlers. It was these settlers who built the present row of houses now existing on our block. At the present time, this area is considered middle class and consists of a mixture of cultures and ethnicity.

One night, Christine and I were sitting on the front steps, talking about this newfound information. One of Karin's friends, Michael, a neighbor's son, was walking by and stopped to chat for a while. We were really feeling great that night, empowered by the recent revelations and looking forward to the forthcoming investigation. So, without much fanfare, we just asked him straight out if he ever had any strange phenomena happen to him.

At first he said, "No," but suddenly changed that to a "Well, yeah, if you count the ghost in my house."

Ghost in his house? We wanted to hear everything, but he seemed a little hesitant to continue. In order to help him feel more at ease we told him a little of what had been going on in our own house and that seemed to make him much more comfortable. I guess it's always easier to feel crazy when you're not the only one!

He sat down next to us and began. "Ever since I was a child, my parents and I have seen a ghost of a little boy in our house. Let's see, I'm twenty-four now, so we've been seeing him for about twenty years. It seems to us that his name is 'Phillip,' so that's what we call him. This ghost is so solid-looking that there were lots of times my father mistook him for me!"

Michael looked at us, then turned away, seeming pleased that we hadn't laughed at him yet, and continued, "I gotta tell you, I'd absolutely cringe under my blanket at night, afraid to look around my room because I was so scared I'd see him. Sometimes he'd move things around in my room and then I'd get blamed for it. I kept telling my mom and dad that it wasn't me doing those things, but they didn't believe me. It took them a few years to understand that I wasn't lying, but that was only after they'd seen him themselves."

Chris and I were listening so intently that the rest of the block seemed to fade in the distance.

"Are you sure you're okay with this?" he said.

We replied, in unison, "Absolutely. Please, tell us what else happened."

He smiled at our response and went on, "Well, we decided to do a little investigating ourselves. We asked around and found out that many years ago a little boy, perhaps five or six years old, had drowned in a well near our property. As far as we knew, there was no well anywhere near our house. But you know how we always put out our decorations at Christmas, the lighted figures of Mary, Joseph and Jesus? Well, three winters ago, during that really big snowstorm, we noticed that they'd sunk into the ground well below where the snow met the dirt in the front yard. When my dad looked at it, he realized that the weight of the snow had caused something underneath to collapse. We got our shovels and dug through the mound of snow, through the hard winter dirt below, and came upon some rotting pieces of wood. Under these strips of wood was a long, dark, empty hole. It was so deep we couldn't see the bottom, not even with flashlights. We filled it up with dirt and snow and put the figures back in place. My mom and dad nearly freaked at the thought that this could be 'the well,' and they won't talk about it. But, I don't know, I would've liked to see what was down there."

We talked for hours that night. He said he'd heard that during the time the farmers lived here it was common to have a well on their property. He really seemed to want to know why this ghost was haunting his house. He seemed more curious than scared, and I admired that. He was enthralled with our stories about our house. He had a strong belief in life after death and he took our stories, and his own, in stride. After a while we said good night and promised to talk again soon.

Of great interest to me was the fact that, just before he left, he said one of his neighbors had also seen the little boy ghost in *his* bedroom. Their houses were on the same side of the street as ours, only a few doors down. I wondered if we could be living in a whole area that was haunted.

Michael's mother Ellen was an acquaintance of mine and I had always enjoyed talking to her. Neither she, nor I, ever mentioned anything like this to each other. So, the next day, when I saw her sitting outside, I went over to talk. I asked her if her son had mentioned our conversation of the previous night.

She looked at me with fear in her eyes. "He told me. I don't like to talk about it. I saw the little boy many times and I get so scared whenever it happens that sometimes I run out of the house. I really don't want to even think about it."

I understood completely. We briefly discussed my house, but I could see it made her very uncomfortable. I changed the subject and we had a nice little chat about ordinary things. I never brought it up to her again. However, she helped me to feel that I wasn't the only person who could be terribly frightened by this sort of experience.

Those last two weeks were filled with new information, but we were still having a hard time piecing it all together. I now had two neighbors I could talk to and this made me feel much less freaky. We were all looking forward to the investigation, looking forward to some real answers. We wanted some peace and tranquility, only this time, not only for ourselves, but for whatever spirits resided with us.

11

February 2, 1995 . . . the big day had arrived. Dr. Holzer and Marisa Anderson were due at our house at 12 P.M. I had stayed up most of the night wondering what to expect, wondering what would be going on in our house in just a few hours. I was very pleased with myself regarding my attitude shift toward this whole affair. I was happy that, at the very least, they might be able to discover who had been making their presence known for so long in our home, and, more importantly, perhaps we could help them. The information acquired in the last few weeks, and the fact that I felt I could talk more freely about the house, enabled me to look forward to this day with curiosity and open-mindedness. Two people were coming to our house who totally accepted that it could be, and probably was, haunted. They didn't think it odd or unusual. I liked that very much, and I liked knowing we might end this day with some actual answers.

My mind felt calmer and clearer and much less full of fear than ever before. My skepticism seemed to blend into the background for a while and I knew I could approach this day with a sense that anything was possible. I was finally able to stop skipping down all the rational caverns of my mind, searching for something on which to hang my hat. I was open and ready and willing to hear whatever they had to say.

I remembered all the terrifying nights, all the interrupted sleep. I thought about the lights and the noises, the odors and the fears. I was still a little scared, but I didn't want to be. I tried to help myself not to be. I did some relaxation exercises and prepared myself to meet this new experience. I finally drifted off about three o'clock in the morning, sleeping soundly in my safe room.

I awakened full of anticipation and hope. Karin and Christine were as excited as I was, so I let them take the day off from school. I imagined writing absence notes for both of them, saying, "Please excuse Karin and Christine from school today due to the fact that their house is being investigated for paranormal activity." That would surely go over well with their teachers! The thought of it made us all laugh. We talked over breakfast about what we were expecting.

"What happens if they find something?" Christine offered. "What do we do then?"

Karin was quick to add, "Well, what if they find nothing? What then?"

"There is no way to know what they'll find," I added, "so why don't we hold off judgment until later today? Let's just see how things go, okay? I know it's weird, having these people over, but they really might provide us with some clues."

"But what are they actually going to do, Mom?" asked Karin. "What if they do something we don't want them to? What if they make things worse, or somehow disturb our spirits?"

I could hear her concern, and I thought it was valid. "I don't have the answers, honey, so why don't we just wait and see. They do this all the time. Let's try to just keep an open mind and hear what they have to say. It's kind of exciting, though, isn't it? Hans Holzer. I remember him from when I was younger and saw him on TV. I'm sure he knows what he's doing."

"Well," she replied, with an air of cynicism that I didn't think she was old enough to express, "I don't know. I'm not sure how I feel about this."

"Are you having reservations? Do you want to call this whole thing off?" I said, hoping she wouldn't call my bluff.

"No, I don't want them not to come. It's just that I'm not comfortable with them snooping around, asking all sorts of questions. I want them to take a look, see whatever they have to see, and then leave."

She hadn't expressed such concern before and I wondered why she waited until a few hours before their arrival to voice her opinion. I had a feeling in my gut that Karin had a lot of genuine feeling for the spirits in our home, and this was her way of being somehow protective of them. "I'm sure everything will be okay," I replied, knowing how hollow that reassurance sounded, "and, before we know it, the day will be over and we might be left with some techniques that can show us how to cope with these things better than we do now."

She looked at me, obviously not satisfied with my answer, and simply said, "Well, I hope so. I hope you're right."

I hoped I was right, too. Christine just listened to our conversation and really didn't seem all that concerned. The dialogue ended and we all took showers, got dressed, and awaited the first of our guests.

Matthew was coming over at 11 A.M., as was Karin's friend, Maria. When they arrived, coffee and bagels were on the table and we all shared our respective feelings of enthusiasm and doubt regarding what was about to occur.

We were all "humming" inside, almost as much as the house was "humming" outside. Interestingly, no actual phenomena occurred that morning. No balls of light, no odd sounds or odors, nothing. Rather, there was a sense of aliveness to the house, a sense of anticipation *outside* of ourselves. Surprisingly, it didn't produce any fear in us, just an aura of excitement.

At twelve o'clock, on the dot, Joe and Maura drove up with Dr. Holzer and Marisa Anderson. My heart leaped as I answered the door. I was really thrilled to meet Dr. Holzer. I knew he'd written quite a few books and I felt honored that he was willing to investigate my house—and that he was willing to do it for free. As he entered my foyer, I noticed that he was a rather distinguished gentlemen, quite tall, with piercing eyes. He was very friendly, and asked me to call him Hans. He was very matter-of-fact, not at all stuffy like I'd feared. He vigorously shook my hand and introduced me to Marisa.

She was a real surprise to me. Without being fully conscious of it until that very moment, I'd expected that she'd be a short, squat, strange-looking woman. That was my foolish image of what a medium looked like. Instead, standing in front of me was a very attractive woman, dressed in a black, one-piece, snug-fitting pants suit, topped with a charcoal blazer. She looked quite normal, her face brightened by a great big smile. She was about my age, and, to my embarrassment, I found myself wishing I could look as good, and as thin, as she did. I silently vowed to myself to stay on my diet, and, for a few moments, even in the midst of all this excitement, became annoyed at myself for having gained fifteen pounds in the last few years.

I quickly turned my attention back to our visitors.

"Here, Elaine, could you save these for later?" Marisa was asking, handing me a box of French pastries. "Usually, after I do a job like this, I get really drained. These provide the perfect pick-me-up when I need some sugar."

French pastries! I couldn't help but envy her ability to eat these things and stay so slim. If I *smell* chocolate, I gain weight!

"No problem," I answered. "We'll have coffee later."

She had a kind smile and bright, sparkling eyes, but I wondered what she might be doing in our house that would cause her to get so drained.

Both Hans and Marisa made themselves comfortable on our living room couch. Everyone introduced themselves and we made small talk, but, in all honesty, it felt very awkward to me. I wasn't sure when we were supposed to talk about the real reason they were here. I asked if anyone wanted to have coffee, thinking we could take that opportunity to turn the conversation into the area of psychic phenomena, into the area of what had been happening in our house for the last twelve years.

Neither one of them was interested in coffee.

"The house feels very 'heavy,' Elaine," Marisa said, her eyes darting from one area of the living room to the other. "I need to get to work immediately. There's a 'vortex' in this room, (just as Maura had stated a few weeks ago), and I think in runs through the floor into a lower level. Do you have a basement? I'd like to go to whatever is down there right now."

She hadn't been in our house for more than five minutes.

I was enthralled and disappointed at the same time. I envisioned us sitting around the dining room table, discussing all the aspects of our problem, and then, after we got to know each other a little, we could begin talking about what had been happening in our house for the last twelve years. I wanted to make some sort of a connection to these people.

Weeks earlier, Joe and I had written a very brief synopsis of the haunting, just a few descriptive lines, to show to Hans and Marisa, to see if they were interested in taking on our house. We hadn't even begun to describe a tenth of what we'd experienced, and we certainly didn't mention the basement, so I was quite surprised when Marisa insisted on going down there.

"Sure, sure, Marisa," I replied. "You can go down to the basement."

As she and Hans got up from their seats, I found myself getting up and opening the front door, looking for their "equipment." I imagined infrared lights and cameras, radioactivity detection devices, and maybe, motion sensors. There was nothing on the front steps, nothing in the hallway. I came back into the living room and noticed that Hans had a camera, but nothing else. All I could think was that they must be very low-tech psychic investigators.

Marisa was becoming insistent on seeing the basement. Joe had brought his video camera, tripod, and lights. As he was fiddling with these things, Marisa had found the basement door and was heading straight down the stairs. We all followed her, backed up by my brother and Matthew lagging slightly behind, trying to get the lights to fit in the basement stairwell. Marisa, almost trance-like, went directly, and I mean *directly*, to the dirt room. No one had to tell her where the nearly invisible doors were located, no one had to tell her how to open them up. She pried them apart, lifted herself up, and sat inside, her head bent to accommodate the low ceiling, and her legs dangling down.

I wouldn't have sat inside there for all the money in the world, yet, there she was, unafraid, sitting right in the middle of what I considered to be the center of all our disturbances.

She didn't care at all that her beautiful pantsuit was now covered with dirt. She sat there quietly, with Hans by her side, for quite some time.

My brother set up his video camera and the lights. We all assembled only a few feet away, near the bottom of the basement stairs. Marisa had her eyes closed, and seemed to be listening to something. We had no idea what she was doing and no explanation was given. We watched and wondered, full of anticipation for whatever was to happen next.

Slowly, she began to speak. In a soft whisper she said, "I'm listening to some entities located in this place. I'm having a little difficulty understanding them."

Very calm. Just like that. Chills began to inch their way up my spine.

Marisa continued, "I think they're speaking Dutch."

More chills. The first settlers in the area were Dutch.

Hans said, "I can speak German. The languages are close so maybe that would help." With that, he became the translator.

He continued, "Someone named 'Estefan' is the prime speaker."

Estefan. Stephen. That was the name of the previous owner's son, the one who died shortly after his bride. When I heard this name, I nearly passed out My brother shot me a look of disapproval, noting that my rather loud gasp would be heard on the video.

Within moments it became clear that this "Estefan" was not the Stephen who lived here in the 1950s. According to Hans, this Estefan had worked on a sort of a railroad track and had been buried alive, in the area below our dirt room, somewhere in the mid- to late-1800s. I felt no sense of relief at this bit of news. All I could think of was that there might be *people buried in our basement.*

Marisa, her eyes continuously closed, perched on the entrance to the dirt room, continued to have what appeared to be a two-way conversation with this spirit known as "Estefan." She would ask Hans to ask the spirit a question in German, then there would be a pause, sometimes for as long as a few minutes. During these pauses she seemed to be trying to hear, or figure out what was being said. Then she would repeat what she heard to Hans and he would translate it into English. Also, during the pause, she would lean her head as far back as she could into the dirt room. We could see her pick up some of the dirt, let it run through her fingers, and then gently pat it down again. Sometimes she seemed to be almost caressing the dirt floor. After a while, Hans started to hear bits of the spirit's conversation, too, and then the translation became faster and clearer.

Matthew, Maura, Christine, Maria, and I were virtually huddled together, transfixed by what we were witnessing. Karin was standing farther away, by herself. She seemed very uncomfortable. Joe was concentrating on getting it all on tape. At no time did any of us hear any spirit voices. We heard only what Hans and Marisa were saying. We were listening intently and we were very quiet.

At one point, about ten minutes into the experience, the whole basement filled with the sweet smell of bananas. I noticed it, but said nothing, and no one else said anything either. Marisa opened her eyes long enough to explain to us that this odor was quite common when spirits were present and it was nothing to worry about. She said this before any of us had acknowledged the smell. We all just looked at each other, not knowing what to think, and went back to focusing our attention on Marisa and Hans.

The apparent dialogue continued. It was very hard for us to understand exactly what was being said. All we could hear were the partners whispering in German and English. This was all being done very quietly, almost reverently.

Marisa opened her eyes for a few moments, as if sensing our frustration, and very peacefully and caringly explained, "I'm sensing five people here who were buried alive, three men and two women. They are buried somewhere under this crawl space's dirt floor. The only names coming through are Estefan, his brother, Michael, and someone named Ranier. I am not getting any of the female names. There were also two dogs buried along with them. It appears that they're saying they were building something on tracks. Not quite a railroad, but something like a mine of some sort. I can see very big bins located on top of two steel, or iron, railings. I sort of feel, and can almost see, that these railings somehow ran through this neighborhood, underneath the basements of the houses. A collapse occurred and they were buried underneath the rubble. I'm sensing they're saying to me that they felt this collapse was either purposefully done, or the result of someone's negligence. This happened somewhere in the mid-1800s. These poor souls have no idea they're dead." She grew silent again and poked her head deeply into the opening of the dirt room.

I had no idea how to react to this information. It was so unexpected, so unnerving, that I said and did absolutely nothing. I simply listened.

She continued, again, very softly, respectfully. "It took some of these spirits as long as five days to die. They'd all been crushed, but remained alive for a few days, and, finally, suffocated to death."

Without thinking, I blurted out, "How can they talk about their death if they don't know they are, indeed, dead?" The reverence was broken. Instinctively lowering my head, I waited for her answer. I couldn't tell if anyone else was looking at me.

"On some level, it appears that they knew, in a way," she replied, "but because their spirits remained so aware, they eventually refused to believe that life had ended for them. They are very confused and quite lost. And they've been pleading for help."

I was not in the frame of mind to question her further. Her explanation seemed plausible to me, so I went back to being silent, and she went back to having her conversation with the entities. All I heard her say next, in an almost childlike tone, after some inaudible mumblings between herself and Hans, was, "You need to know that you are dead. You have been dead for a very, very long time and we're here to help you now. Just understand that you are dead. And we can help you." She repeated this a few times.

The basement was so thick with silence it was getting hard to breathe. We were all so still, I imagined that we looked somewhat frozen in time. Soon came the response.

Marisa brought her head out into the open and said, "They've been trying to communicate to you what happened here. Don't get upset, but they did mention you by name." According to Marisa, they actually vocalized: "Karin, Christine, and Elaine."

And she said they were very angry. They couldn't understand how much time had passed since their horrible accident. All they knew was that they were desperate for relief and had no idea what to do.

I felt my skepticism trying to rise to the surface—this was a lot to swallow. But my heart pushed it away. At that point, and without wanting to, I found myself crying. All I could imagine was how awful it must have been for these entities, buried alive, stuck in a time warp, trying to find their way out. I started to feel so sorry for all the fear I'd felt for so many years. They weren't evil, they were in pain.

Hans snapped me out of my thoughts by announcing, "They've been trying to communicate their feelings as best they could. They've been letting you feel what they last felt. Pressure. Immobility. Suffocation."

He continued describing their sensations, but I didn't hear him clearly anymore. As I looked around the room, searching the faces of my loved ones and friends, I felt my mind go numb. Thoughts came slowly and they came painfully. I remembered all those times I was pushed into my bed, surrounded by feelings of anger and rage and desperation. I relived those awful moments and felt very frightened. I moved closer to Matthew.

"My chest feels very heavy, Elaine. The air is thick in here," he said.

"Are you having chest pains?" I asked him anxiously, in true nursing form.

"No, no, nothing like that. Don't worry. It's just that the atmosphere in here is so laden with . . . something."

He left it at that and gave me a hug. I looked at the the others. They appeared dismayed and sad and shocked and scared, all at the same time. We spontaneously all held hands. It helped.

Karin seemed to be getting upset. Not in a sad way, but in an angry one. I didn't ask her why. It didn't seem appropriate just then. I observed her and turned my attention back to the medium.

As Marisa continued her dialogue she related to us that the spirits told her they absolutely hated rodents of any kind. Rats had picked at and tortured them. I couldn't help but remember Karin's gerbil cage experience. I asked Marisa to ask them if gerbils fell into the rodent category. A resounding "yes" was perceived by her. Then, while lowering her eyes, she said they felt sorry if they'd caused any harm.

I needed a breather. As the conversations went on, I backed off a little. I looked at this whole picture and felt an utter sense of unreality. Joe was tensely peering into his video camera, making minor adjustments and lighting changes as needed.

Once in a while he'd give us a quick glance and slightly raise his eyebrows, as if to say, "This is incredible, isn't it?" It was such an endearing expression.

Except for Marisa, perched at the entrance to the dirt room, no one else was seated. Hans was standing next to her, with Joe standing near them. Matthew, Maura, Christine, and Maria were standing very close to each other, all of them leaning forward ever so slightly, paying close attention. Karin was standing farther back, looking displeased and angry, arms folded across her chest. I started to approach her, but she took a few steps back and I knew, at that point, that she did not want to talk.

Observing all this, the banana odor still lingering in the air, I became aware of the normal day-to-day, neighborhood noises. Cars going by, people talking. The world outside seemed so far away from the unfolding drama going on in our basement. I felt very detached. I was more comfortable when I was part of the group, so I nuzzled next to Matthew again and tried to focus on what was happening.

Hans and Marisa became very quiet. Both their eyes were closed and they seemed to be preparing for something. We waited, holding our breaths, wondering what would happen next. Marisa began to speak, Hans translating every word. She told these spirits that they had to "go to the light." She repeated over and over again that they had been dead for many years and they needed to let go and find "the light."

It dawned on me, right at that moment, that she was "cleaning" our house. That had not been part of the deal. It had not even been mentioned. We were ready for an investigation, ready for some answers, but this took us by surprise. I felt a sensation of fullness in my chest, and I was absolutely thrilled by this new turn of events. All I could think of was how wonderful it would be if it actually worked. I wondered if they actually could do this. When I turned to the others, they seemed happy and excited as well. But when I looked at Karin, she seemed angrier than ever.

I moved closer to her, and she stood her ground, so, in a whisper, I spoke, "Karin, what's wrong? Why are you so upset?"

She just glared at me and refused to say a word. I knew we hadn't talked about having the house "cleaned" just yet, and I knew we hadn't expected it to happen today. She refused another attempt on my part to talk to her. I backed off, but, somehow, I got the sense that Karin felt betrayed.

Once again, my attention was drawn to Marisa. She was telling the spirits to call out to their parents or anyone else who had loved them in this life. After repeating this perhaps ten times, everything became very silent. It stayed that way for what seemed like five or ten minutes. No one spoke a word. All I could hear was the different and varying rhythms of everyone's breathing. Then, slowly, softly, she spoke, "Can you see the light?"

Hans, just as softly, repeated the question in German. They paused again.

Then Marisa, her head deep within the entrance, said, "They can see it. They can see it and they want to go."

Hans approvingly clapped his hands together once and smiled. We were in awe of the whole process.

Marisa positioned herself even deeper inside the dirt room. We couldn't see her head or left hand, which she was using to brace herself in that uncomfortable position. Her torso and legs were visible, and she was using her right hand to guide the spirits to the "light." She was making smooth, "ushering" movements, like someone conducting a flowing musical piece. She would make these wavelike hand motions, then grow silent, then do them again. When she'd move a little, and we could manage to get a momentary glimpse of her face, her eyes were closed, her expression strained. She looked like she was in a state of total concentration. Hans never left her side and he, too, seemed almost to be in prayer.

This went on for nearly three hours. I don't remember getting fidgety, don't remember anyone leaving to go to the bathroom or have a drink of water. We stood there, watching, absorbing this powerful scene.

I became aware that there was no longer any banana odor, and the atmosphere in the basement became light and airy. This happened in an instant. Within moments, Marisa jumped down from her perch and announced that, one by one, with their two dogs, the spirits had left and gone to the "light." Except for Karin, we were all crying.

They were gone. We could feel it. I had no idea what to expect next.

Marisa looked absolutely exhausted. Hans seemed to fare a little better, and I watched as he animatedly spoke to Joe, talking to him about video equipment.

After Marisa dusted herself off, I asked if it might be a good time to serve those pastries she'd brought, but she declined. "I'm not through yet. I need to feel out the rest of the house."

"Please, Marisa, you seem so tired. Let's have coffee now, and you can explore some more later. Let's just sit down for a while." I was speaking as much for the others as for myself. We were tired. We wanted a break.

"Elaine, I can't," she explained. "The vortex might have a few more spirits in it and I need to do a full house cleaning."

With that, she wanted to go upstairs to the first floor, so we all accompanied her. Joe set up his video camera and we watched her immediately head for my original bedroom, the cheese-box, in the back of the house.

She sat on my bed, closed her eyes, and said, "I sense a presence here and I'm getting the name 'George.' I sort of feel nauseous, and I'm having some difficulty breathing."

Sitting on my bed, she grew very quiet, and, once again, started those ushering hand movements. There was no conversation this time. Hans was by her side, taking an occasional picture, nodding empathetically when she voiced her discomfort. I watched her mouth a silent prayer as she guided this spirit, too, to the light.

When she was done, I spoke up. "Who was George?" I asked, "Was he the one who kept bothering me in this room?"

"I think not," she said, turning to Hans for confirmation. "The spirits who were in the basement were the ones communicating with you here."

"But what about the sexual overtones I felt in that bed? Sometimes I'd feel my thighs or arms beings stroked."

Hans laughed slightly as he responded, "I got the impression that one of the men buried downstairs was 'playful' in that way. He meant no harm."

I kept quiet, but I didn't like the sound of that, and I wasn't sure why. It felt like an almost flippant answer to what had been so very tortuous for me. I wondered how much of all of this I was willing to accept.

When Marisa left that bedroom she walked right past Christine's old room, my present sanctuary. I wondered if she'd venture in there, but she stopped at the door and indicated that there was no need. She said, quite nonchalantly, "This room was not here when those poor souls were buried alive, so they didn't recognize it's existence."

Goose bumps, once again, rose from the root of my spine all the way up to my head. They had no way of knowing that it was a late addition to the house, and they had no way to know it was my safe haven.

I gathered myself together and joined the others in continuing to follow Hans and Marisa, who paused at the bathroom. She gave it a quick "feel," and then stood for a moment in the kitchen.

"These rooms are clear," she stated, "but when I stand near the stove, I feel like I could walk right through it and I don't understand why."

But, incredibly, I understood. When we first bought the house, there had been two entrances to the kitchen. One was by the bathroom, and the other, where the stove was. We needed more cabinet space, so we closed this entrance off and had the whole kitchen redesigned. The stove and the cabinets above it now were right where the old entrance used to be. The work had been done at least ten years ago and there were no signs whatsoever that an entrance had ever existed there. I explained this to Marisa and it seemed to make her very happy. I, on the other hand, was truly taken aback by her insight. It helped me to believe in what was going on.

She moved on to the dining room and sat quietly again. Eyes closed. Very serious facial expression. Then she got up and said, "I know you had a lot of frightening experiences here, but it was just symptomatic of a problem somewhere else in the house. The vortex is still open in the living room, but don't be concerned. We'll be dealing with that a little later. I sense no spirits here. Hans and I want to see the second floor."

We let them lead the way and followed right behind, while Joe and Matthew struggled again with the video and lighting equipment.

The atmosphere in the house that day had been so charged, almost electric. We'd all been almost school-girl nervous about the whole thing. But now, about five hours later, we felt sort of solemn. Quiet. Tired. We had a lot of information to digest and we weren't talking too much amongst ourselves. I knew Karin was going through some sort of struggle with this, but she wouldn't talk about it. To her credit, she managed to remain very cordial to our guests. I didn't know what to think, or what to feel. I went from doubt to belief, from fear to relief. It was indeed a very strange day, and it didn't look like it was over yet.

Once on the second floor, Hans and Marisa marched right up to the entrance of Christine's present bedroom. They shared a look of confusion and agreement, then Marisa said, "We feel like we have to stop here, like there's nothing beyond that doorway. Almost like there's a wall in front of us." Again, I understood.

Christine's new bedroom was also an addition to the house, and I told them so. Hans said there wouldn't be any necessity for a cleansing in there either. We moved briefly through the dining room and neither of them felt any inclination to stop. However, then they entered the front room, my previous bedroom.

"My dear, what are you feeling now? I'm aware of some heaviness here," Hans said to Marisa, who was standing in the middle of the room, head bowed.

"Just some negative energy. I need to stay here for a few moments."

We all crowded in the doorway and watched her. She stood perfectly still, both she and Hans had their eyes closed. Then Marisa spoke, "What we're feeling here is nothing more than shadows of those unfortunate beings from the basement. It'll dissipate soon and shouldn't cause you any more trouble."

We were finally able to take our last trek of the day, up to the third floor—Karin's bedroom. We all sat on her bed, except for Joe. Again, Hans and Marisa seemed to almost go into a trance.

After a few moments, Marisa stated, "I believe someone died in this room—by their own hand. I sense a female presence who had been rather 'unbalanced' and very unhappy during her life here on Earth. She was extremely small in stature and very, very frightened."

The "little lady." I told them what we knew of her: that she died shortly after her wedding of an apparent heart attack or cerebral aneurysm. Marisa felt very strongly that she had committed suicide, but there was, of course, no way to prove her right or wrong. She asked for a moment of silence and began the now familiar ritual of ushering this spirit to the "light." There was no dialogue between her or Hans and this spirit. The only time they did that three-way conversation was in the basement.

After a few minutes, she said the spirit had gone. And, once again, like downstairs, the atmosphere in Karin's room became lighter, brighter, and fear-free.

We moved on to the other two rooms. In the third one, the one Karin used for storage, Marisa sensed that three children had died in a fire, in a tenement building that used to be where our house is now. Nothing in the Hall of Records had indicated a fire, or a tenement. I told her we sometimes heard the giggling of children, but that was the only connection I could make. Without solid evidence, it is impossible to substantiate what someone senses. She bowed her head in prayer and guided these spirits, too, to the light.

She then turned to us with a tired smile on her face, and said, "Your house is now clean."

Hans gave us all a big hug. I was not aware of feeling anything in particular at that moment. I was disappointed that I was not overjoyed, not particularly pleased, neither happy nor unhappy.

Exhausted, we all went downstairs to the first floor dining room to have coffee and those delicious-looking French pastries. Nearly six hours had passed by. It was now early evening, but there was so much snow on the ground outside, it still appeared, through the windows, to be daytime.

Marisa looked very tired and drawn, like her energy had been almost completely depleted. She was quiet and remote. Hans was still talkative, still energetic and friendly. I served the coffee and pastry, and for the first ten minutes or so there was total silence at the table. Joe was concluding his taping and Hans was checking his camera. We all stared at each other, not knowing what to say.

I spoke up first. "I was astonished at the accuracy of some of your findings," I said. "A lot of it coincides with what we found in the Hall of Records and with my conversations with some of my neighbors. I was impressed especially with your description of the 'little lady.' It gave me the chills when you said she was so small. But the prospect that there might be actual bodies—well, bones by now—below our basement is a little unnerving. The whole day was unnerving."

Hans said, sipping his coffee, "It's a lot to absorb in such a small amount of time. I've been to many other houses and everyone reacts differently. Give yourself a few weeks to understand what happened here."

Marisa was silent, looking like she felt uneasy.

I smiled at him graciously, but, inside, I was thinking that I really had no idea what had happened here. And he was right about taking time to absorb it all. Everyone else started talking and, as strange as I thought it was at the time, the conversation was quite normal. Perhaps we needed to get involved with small talk after such an odd and exhausting day. Within a short period of time, we were actually laughing, that is, everyone except Marisa. She remained very quiet, slowly eating her beloved pastries. Then, abruptly, she stood up.

"I need to be by myself in the basement," she said, "also in the back bedroom, the living room, and Karin's room on the third floor. The vortex wasn't completely closed and I want to make sure this is done. It's got to be totally sealed off because, even though I'm positive we sent all those spirits to the light, other spirits could enter through the vortex. It's kind of like a pathway—a conduit used by spirits to enter and leave this world. I don't want anything else to come into your home."

She was making me very nervous, and I had absolutely no inclination to stop her from doing what she felt needed to be done. I was grateful for her thoroughness.

She left the table and spent another hour or so, by herself, making sure no future entry through the vortex was possible.

I hadn't learned about the vortex in my class on the paranormal. I didn't learn about a lot of the things I experienced that day. It was like hearing a new language or gaining entrance into some previously unknown reality. Hans and Marisa took all this stuff for granted—it was normal for them. Maura, too, had psychic abilities and she observed everything that day in a state of understanding, not surprise. Although I was still talking and laughing at the table, I couldn't help but be aware that there was this woman wandering around our house, closing an unseen vortex so other spirits couldn't enter and haunt us, and no one questioned this or gave it much notice.

All bets were off that day. Reality, as I thought I knew it, was on vacation.

Marisa returned and said she was successful. She seemed much more relaxed. She and Hans decided to stay for another cup of coffee, so our conversation continued. I admitted to them how skeptical I could be, how frightened, how I might still doubt what they did and what they said. I told them it took me years to even say the word "haunted."

Hans responded, laughing. "We hear that all the time and it's no surprise to us. Even in the midst of obvious poltergeist activity, some people will still stand there and try to rationalize the whole thing."

That second coffee session produced many more questions. I think we were all a little more relaxed then. I wanted to know who the ghost was that Christine saw on the steps. They said they didn't know for sure, but the previous owner's son might be a good bet. I got nervous again.

"But you didn't sense him, so you didn't send him to the light. How do we know he's gone?" I asked. "And who hit Karin with that clip?"

Then Christine spoke up, "And what about those balls of light, and those dark shapes going in and out of the corners? And what about 'the Mist'?"

Before long, we were bombarding them with questions. Then Hans spoke to us, very politely, "Look, we don't have all the answers. Those balls of light and the shapes are what we refer to as 'discarnate spirits,' spirits without a body. But we don't know what all those different manifestations represented. I wish I could be more specific, but I can't."

I appreciated their honesty, but it made me worry that perhaps they didn't do such a thorough job after all, and I expressed this feeling.

"The psychic door was closed, Elaine, and nothing is left of whatever spirits were here," Marisa explained. "It's not so important to 'catch' each individual spirit, as long as a cleansing was performed. Everything is going to be fine. You'll see."

I certainly hoped so.

The time came for them to leave. It was about nine o'clock in the evening. They said we could call upon them anytime we felt anything out of the ordinary. Marisa said, if necessary, she could even help us over the telephone.

As I watched them get into my brother's car, I couldn't help but feel a great deal of respect for them. It couldn't be easy dealing with something so politically incorrect as a haunting. I wished I could be more sure of what I knew to be true instead of trying to fit my truth into a more acceptable way of thinking.

Everyone had to go to work the next day, and Matthew had to be on his ambulance in only two hours, so we didn't get a chance to talk together about what had happened that day. I was fine with that because I thought we were all pretty much talked out anyway. Karin, Christine, and I said goodbye to everyone and sat down in the living room. We wondered aloud if any activity would present itself that night—or would it just stop? Karin said she was very upset at Marisa and Hans for surprising us with a house-cleaning and not just an investigation.

None of us had the energy to pursue any particular line of thought on the matter. We went to bed shortly after everyone left. We had no concrete idea about what to expect next from our house.

12 The days following our "house-cleaning" passed quite normally. The excitement had disappeared, aptly replaced by a wary vigilance. We didn't know what to expect or what to believe. The house was exceptionally quiet, but it was also like this during our many breaks from activity. We did acknowledge that things felt different somehow. The house felt lighter, less troubled, but this was much too subjective a feeling to convince us that any permanent alteration had taken place.

We talked a lot about what happened, still had many questions, and felt remorseful that we hadn't cleared them up with our visitors. With everything that occurred that day, we forgot to mention M-ow's strange behavior or Christine's water episodes. We didn't tell them about the changing odors in our dining room and we didn't elaborate on our feelings of being watched or the phantom photocopy machine, or the loud banging noises we'd heard upstairs.

I had a great desire to have everything mapped out for me. I wanted every instance of paranormal activity explained in detail, with individual reasons given for each. I still felt in the dark about much of what happened in our house. I was not at all ready to let down my guard.

As in previous vacations from activity in the house, we began to relax a little, but sometimes we still found ourselves sleeping together in the living room. The only difference was that we did this because of a memory of some unpleasant occurrence, rather than as a reaction to an actual incident. We still kept the lights and the TV on, and I continued to sleep, fully clothed, in my safe room. We kept waiting for something to happen.

Karin, I think, was the only one who seemed to almost *want* something to happen. She didn't verbalize this, but it was a feeling I was getting from her. She wasn't very talkative about it, but I did approach her one day.

"You still seem uneasy about the house being cleaned, Karin. Why is that? Aren't you glad that they seem to be gone?"

She looked up at me, not as angrily as I expected her to be. "It's just that I feel it would have been nice to choose whether or not we wanted the activity here to stop. Everyone just assumed it was negative, but that wasn't my experience at all. And I'm not clear about what is still here or not here. Whatever it was, I never saw any malevolence to it, any real reason to 'clean it out.' I would have liked to investigate it more, probe into the area, explore. It was just so fascinating."

I replied honestly, "It just scared me so much of the time, I didn't even stop to think about how fascinating it all was. I just wanted it gone."

She continued, "I know you got scared a lot, and I did, too, sometimes, but if you stop to think about it, we had the opportunity here to delve into something unknown—something amazing. I'm sure I would not have agreed to have the psychic investigators over if I thought they were going to do the cleaning that day. Maybe there were other options, who knows? I just would have liked to have had a say in it, that's all."

I respected her opinion very much, but at the same time I knew I'd never have had the kind of objectivity she was demonstrating. She was more interested in the "why" of it all, in the "what" of it all, as opposed to my reaction of almost complete fear.

She would have been willing to live with our situation and explore it. I wanted it stopped. Even though I did feel compassion toward these entities near the end, in my heart I still had fear. And it was fear that propelled my actions.

I was more than willing to give up any opportunity to "explore" our situation further in exchange for a more normal life in our house. Now I knew Karin was not. I didn't know whether to hope they were gone, or, for Karin's sake, hope that they lingered here still.

To further confuse the issue, the house felt eerily abandoned. Hollow. When any of us were alone in the house, we felt really *alone* in the house. No sense of something there remained. No feeling of being watched, no awareness of someone else with us. As unpleasant as it always was to have a presence perceived by us, it really did feel lonely now. It was nearly as uncomfortable as when we were accompanied.

Christine was happy with the thought that the spirits might be gone, but she, too, could see Karin's point. However, I think that Chris's level of fear was closer to mine, whereas Karin had always been more accepting, and tolerant, of our ghosts. It was a strange time for all of us, and thoughts and feelings were surfacing that were both unexpected and unwelcome.

I found myself thinking about life after death and how our house had affected my views. For many years I stubbornly refused to believe in anything beyond this reality, and scoffed at ghost stories, even as I crept into my safe room. Now, I wasn't so sure anymore. My mind drifted back to that day in February. I remembered watching in awe as the medium mentioned, and probed, areas of our house, and our lives, that she had no prior knowledge of. I thought of how she ushered all those spirits to the "light." Now that some time had passed, and the thrill of that day was gone, I was left with wondering about what exactly happened that day, and what the implications were.

Before we knew it, a full year had gone by. Karin and Christine were doing well in their respective schools and I was still working in the ER. My relationship with Matthew had blossomed into a full-blown love affair. And, incredibly, the house had been completely quiet for the whole time. The fact was that, so far, nothing even vaguely paranormal had happened. Nothing. I began to give credence to what was apparently becoming nonnegotiable—the house-cleaning had worked. I couldn't explain it, and for a while at least I wanted to enjoy it, so, quite consciously, I closed my mind off to the many questions trying to push their way to the surface.

For the first time in years, I relaxed when I came home. We all complained less about feeling tired or having headaches or just feeling out of whack. We began to believe it was finally over. After all this time, it was exciting to think that we'd be able to enjoy our home. It was such a liberating thought. I bought new drapes and sheets and repainted some of the rooms. We had pleasant dinners, enjoyed having guests over, and some of them even stayed overnight. It was as though we were given permission to go on with the rest of our lives. Like we had put in our time, done our duty, and could look to the future with hope and joy. For a while, I didn't want to talk about what happened in our house. I wanted to fully immerse myself in the feeling of not being afraid.

Karin and Christine were sleeping, every night, in their own bedrooms. I returned to my cheese-box and, to my surprise, felt completely at ease there. I even slept in pajamas, with my feet sticking out of the covers, for the first time in years. It might have been a small victory for some, but for me to let my feet show out of the blanket, without fear that a spirit would touch one of my toes, was a major accomplishment. It was indicative of a sense of relaxation I hadn't felt in so long. To me, it meant freedom and it meant safety.

I didn't want to let go of this sense of security. I wanted it to be like in the movies.

Family moves in—finds out house is haunted—"ghost-busters" get rid of them—everything goes back to normal—end of story. But, I knew, even though our ghosts seemed to be gone, in their wake they left some heavy-duty questions. I hoped the house remained comfortable as we began to deal with the ramifications of our experience.

My daughters and I began to feel like we belonged to some exclusive club for members who had not only experienced some sort of psychic phenomena, but who understood that all that seems to be is not all that is. The most fascinating question was brought up by Karin. She wondered if the phenomena was really gone, or, if we just *perceived* it as gone. I wasn't able to deal directly with that thought for quite a while.

I focused on my own questions, and the dichotomy they produced within me. On the one hand, I felt a sense of gratefulness that we were given the opportunity to see, firsthand, a marvelous representation of the unknown. On the other hand, I was angry that we had to be subjected to such fear for so many years. I became anxious and worried, wondering if, indeed, everything was okay now, or, were we to be surprised by some psychic phenomena sometime in the near future. I remembered reading about the training of rats. When scientists put rats in a maze and always shocked them when they made a certain turn, the rats learned how to avoid that particular area of the maze. However, when they randomly shocked them, the rats became extremely stressed because they never knew when, or where, the shock would come. That's how I felt.

My belief systems were getting very shaken up. I always believed in God, even when I didn't believe in life after death. In my mind and heart, God was within me, within everyone. After years of struggling with, and eventually rejecting, the church dogma I had grown up with, I concluded that God was, indeed, the embodiment of love and compassion and those attributes were expressed through our behavior. I believed in the power of prayer, in the power in all of us to help each other through this life.

I was especially bothered by a metaphor used by the medium. When I asked her why these spirits couldn't go to the light on their own, she said that being dead and lost was like being in a pond covered by ice. The person remains trapped, floating underneath the surface, unable to break out without the help of someone living. How awful, and how unbelievably cruel that seemed to me. I did not believe that God would leave His or Her spirits to drown for eternity in such a place, waiting for someone to lead them out. In our case, according to the medium, these poor souls were wandering about in some spiritual morass for over a hundred years, not knowing how to find the light. I refused to acknowledge this as a viable possibility. I believe whatever beings were in our house remained earthbound in some way, and I think they interacted with us, but I couldn't swallow the "ice pond theory." To me, this was just a convenient explanation for the ultimately unexplainable.

I also had my doubts about the vortex. I didn't know if there was such a thing, or, if so, perhaps it was not so cut-and-dried. It was explained to us as an area that allows spirits to enter, or exit, our world. I don't think that anyone, not even psychics or mediums, know exactly how this works. It must be much more convoluted than that, much more complicated. It might be comforting to think that we have some speculative explanation, but I don't know if we have to do this. I didn't understand what would be wrong with simply trusting the fact that we had no pat answers, and just view whatever it was with a sense of mystery and awe.

I went to bed every night hoping that I wouldn't awaken to a suffocating dream, hoping that when I was alone, I wouldn't start hearing footsteps, seeing lights, or hearing muffled voices again. The thought that I *might* kept up the anxiety level. From my studies in psychology, I felt I was suffering a version of post-traumatic stress syndrome. Sometimes only a memory of some of the phenomena would send me, blanket in hand, to sleep in my safe room, even though danger no longer existed.

It bothered me a great deal that I couldn't understand why Hans and Marisa were so successful at clearing our house of spirits. I didn't know how they did what they did. I only knew they did it. I even wondered for a time if they, in some way, hypnotized us. During the course of my nursing career, when I was working with cancer patients, I took special classes and became a certified clinical hypnotherapist. I found hypnotherapy a useful tool in helping people cope with high levels of stress. I was well aware of the induction techniques and suggestions that are the mainstay of hypnosis. Nothing like that had taken place that February day.

With hypnosis ruled out, it was time to deal with Karin's question. What if our ability to perceive the paranormal had been impaired? What if everything was still going on, but we couldn't see it, or hear it or feel it? The thought made me cringe inside. Karin, and then Christine, seemed to embrace this possibility as the most plausible explanation. I, however, could not. I knew Hans and Marisa did their job, and they did it well. I don't know how they did it, but somehow they knew how to help whatever spirits or energies were present in our home.

It was true that I didn't agree with many of their explanations, but I felt those conclusions were simply their attempts at making sense out of the ununderstandable. I had no problem being grateful to both of them despite the gaps in logic presented by some of their arguments. I became content with knowing that something was in our house, something was no longer there, and they got rid of it.

Speaking only for myself, I had no sensation of having had my perceptions tampered with. However, there was something about this possibility that allowed me to understand further that there was no real answer. There didn't have to be a real answer. If Marisa's and Hans' abilities had to do with unwittingly making us unaware of psychic phenomena, then that was one answer. If they, indeed, ushered lost souls to the light, then that, too, was an answer. The whole realm of psychic phenomena was so unclear, so mysterious, so understudied, how could anyone know the absolute truth? It was enough to know that our experience had been genuine and we had gotten a glimpse, however differing our opinions, of another world. The most beautiful part of this was, once that other world was acknowledged, the implications were boundless.

We were free to know, for sure, that there was something else out there, something existing way beyond our everyday reality. My heart filled with gratitude at having been able to experience just a small part of that wondrous truth. Also, if what I believed was so, we had helped some lost souls enter the realm in which they belonged. With all the doubts and all the fears, the whole experience had turned out to be a positive one.

My daughters, too, were content to not know exactly what had happened. Our conversations were sprinkled with this theory or that theory, but we agreed to disagree and focus on how incredible it was that anything happened here at all. It opened our minds and our hearts to all sorts of possibilities.

Our house became a real home. It was warm and friendly and quiet. My anxiety decreased rapidly, knowing now that nothing was coming back to threaten us. I had no hesitation about going downstairs alone to do the laundry. No more trips to the laundromat, no more excuses for a week's build-up of underwear and towels. I was no longer "laundry-challenged"! My nights in my old bedroom were never peppered by any suffocating dreams. Karin had not had one either, not since the day before our house was cleaned. We have grown accustomed to feeling, and enjoying, being completely alone in the house, without any presence felt, or any other uncomfortable sensation, for that matter. My daughters both report the same level of peace that I feel. It was like a new life here, the way I wanted it from the beginning, only its richer and fuller than I ever could have imagined.

Sometimes a memory would come rushing by, touched by a little of the fear I used to feel. It was becoming easier and easier to bypass such a thought. Recently, I went into the garage to get something and I remembered the Bible and the palm. When we were sitting around the dining room table, after Hans and Marisa finished their task, I mentioned what we'd found to Marisa. She donned her heavy winter coat and went with us to investigate the garage. After a few moments, she pronounced the garage clear. She said a grave did not exist there. Rather, it was an area of prayer, perhaps attended to by a former owner who had experienced some of the phenomena and did not know what to make of it. She said the place where the Bible and the palm rested was an area of reverence.

I looked toward that area now and felt no fear at all. I wondered if the person who did the praying had also had a hard time living in our house. I closed the garage door and looked forward to going back inside our home. No longer just a remembered burden, our experience reminded me daily that life truly does go on. It unlocked doors for all of us, opening each one just enough to let our minds wander in and behold little bits of truth.

Epilogue

It is now April of 1999. Four years and two months have passed since our visit from the psychic investigators. Matthew and I were married in October, 1997. Karin and Christine are both in college and involved in their own relationships. We still live in the house. The house remains, for the most part, free of any paranormal activity.

We don't talk too much any more about what happened, although we certainly haven't forgotten. We look upon it as a unique time in our lives. However, my daughters are completely comfortable with the house's past and are able to put it behind them much more comfortably than I can.

Although I still believe the experience had a positive influence in our lives, and I can recognize that it had something to do with both of my children growing up to be, in my admittedly biased opinion, particularly intelligent, creative, and open-minded individuals, for me it has not been such smooth sailing.

Some of the fear remains. I think I'm still suffering from some sort of psychic post-traumatic stress syndrome. Writing this book was difficult, with memories of the haunting enough to still frighten me. Sitting at my computer, day after day, putting all this together, I found it difficult to write in the nighttime and impossible if I was alone in the house. As I saw our experiences appear in print on the screen in front of me, I was forced to relive some of the more upsetting feelings, most clearly the suffocating dreams. The memory of it is certainly not the same as the real thing, but still unnerving. Matthew eyes that upstairs front bedroom with desire, but he is patient with the fact that I insist we sleep in the tiny cheese-box down-

171

stairs. The horrible nights I spent in that room upstairs are still too clear in my mind.

When I am able to push the fear aside, I remain grateful. What happened in our house has opened my mind to so many possibilities. I no longer limit myself to assuming that my everyday reality is all that exists. I no longer doubt the validity of our haunting, nor do I need to understand all of its nuances. I know that if it could happen to us then it could happen to anyone. The most important implication of all is that it has enabled me to listen to the experiences of others without prejudging them.

I have heard people talk about extraterrestrials, out-of-body states, alien abductions, seeing fairies, having near-death experiences—whatever. I don't necessarily believe all of them, but I will discount none of it. For me now, it is all conceivable, and some of it probable. This slant on things is directly related to our haunting, and for that I will be forever in its debt. In many ways, it was, indeed, well worth the fear. It is amazing for me to understand that "unexplainable" no longer has to mean "nonexistent."

About two years ago, we had a little paranormal scare. We thought it might be a tease that things were going to perk up again. I was awakened at six o'clock in the morning by the ringing of our doorbell. I was startled out of sleep and apprehensive because of the early time. As I walked to the door, I remembered that Matthew was asleep in our bedroom, my daughters were upstairs, and I had spoken only hours ago to my brother and my parents. I felt calmer knowing it couldn't be bad news about any one of them. When I went to open the door, I looked through the peephole first. Standing at the front gate, about eight feet from our front door, was what looked like a policeman, but he was wearing a more casual uniform—a dark blue sweater and slacks.

He was leaning on the gate and, as hard as I stared through that peephole, I could not make out his face. I did not open the door. I watched him for a few minutes, waiting to see if he'd approach the door again to ring the bell, still not being able to identify his face. But, he just stood there, motionless. Then, as I watched, he slowly *dissolved*. He sort of melted into the dawn, into the shadow of our tree.

I was not overly frightened by this and I'm not sure why. I went back to bed, and in the morning, told Matthew about what happened. We thought it odd, and silently, I worried that things might be happening again. A few days went by and then Matthew said he sensed a young male presence upstairs. I went up there, but did not feel anything. We decided to pray for this spirit. We prayed that he would find the "light." Two or three days later, while I lay sleeping by his side, Matthew was awakened by our doorbell, also at six o'clock in the morning. He didn't answer the ring—he waited for it to ring again. It didn't. He said he had a strong feeling it was this same spirit, leaving. He has not come back. I was greatly relieved it was not an indication of further activity.

The only other small problem we've had is, ironically, in that little room that used to be my safe haven. The twin bed is now pushed to the side, and my computer and desk take up the rest of the room. After a long evening of writing, I decided to take a nap for a while, and snuggled myself into the bed. I was awakened by a sensation of being poked, or tapped, on my shoulder. Memories came flooding back, and I've refused to rest there again. Also, when Matthew was napping in there, with the door closed, I walked by to go to the bathroom and heard something slam against the door, hard, as if a significant weight had been tossed at it. I stood there, unable to yell for Matthew to get up, but he woke up anyway. He heard the noise, but the source was not identifiable. I am content to just avoid sleeping in that room, and, as long as it doesn't get worse, I'm okay writing in there when I'm not alone in the house, or when it is daytime.

All of us have felt strange at times, almost seeing things from the corners of our eyes, detecting some movement just outside our vision. Compared to what we used to experience, this is nothing. We've chalked it up to the stirrings of memory and basically just leave it alone. I have only two rules that reflect what we've been through. One, I won't allow the dirt room doors to be opened and two, I don't want a Ouija board brought into the house.

I still think my children would like all the activity to return, but I don't have any such nostalgia. I am content to appreciate what it gave us, and appreciate that it is gone.

If it were to come back full force, I don't think I could ever go through that again. I know I could not.

It is my hope that this book can comfort other people who are having difficulty coming out of their haunting "closet." I want them to know they're not alone and that many families have gone through this ordeal and survived intact.

Most importantly, I want this book to convey the hope that there is life after death—that in some form or other, we go on. I went for years lost in the feeling that when we died there was nothing left but dust. Not anymore. I can't ignore the significance of the various spirits who manifested themselves in our home. We, and others, were there. We saw them and heard them—and felt them. They proved to me, without a doubt, that we survive our physical death. I don't claim to know how this is, or why this is, I just know that it is.

It is my hope that this book can help some readers reach the same conclusion. It is also my sincere wish that our experiences will be believed.

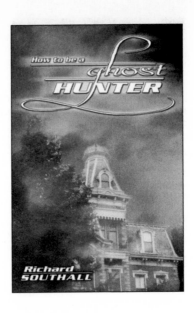

HOW TO BE A GHOST HUNTER

Richard Southall

So you want to investigate a haunting? This book is full of practical advice used in the author's own ghost- hunting practice. Find out whether you're dealing with a ghost, spirit, or an entity . . . and discover the one time when you should stop what you're doing and call in an exorcist. Learn the four-phase procedure for conducting an effective investigation, how to capture paranormal phenomena on film, record disembodied sounds and voices on tape, assemble an affordable ghost-hunting kit, and form your own paranormal group.

For anyone with time and little money to spend on equipment, this book will help you maintain a healthy sense of skepticism and thoroughness while you search for authentic evidence of the paranormal.

- Written by a paranormal investigator with fifteen years of experience, focusing on practical advice
- The only handbook that details how to form paranormal groups, research a suspected haunted area, and practice effective eyewitness interview techniques.
- Provides contact information on paranormal organizations and supply warehouses for hard-to-find materials (electromagnetic detectors, infrared film, etc.)

0-7387-0312-5, 5⅜ x 8, 216 pp., photos   **$12.95**

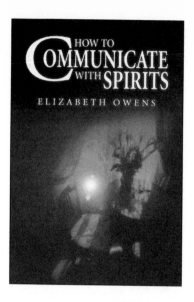

HOW TO COMMUNICATE
WITH SPIRITS

Elizabeth Owens

Spiritualist mediums share their fascinating experiences with the "other side" . . .

No where else will you find such a wealth of anecdotes from noted professional mediums residing within a Spiritualist community. These real-life psychics shed light on spirit entities, spirit guides, relatives who are in spirit, and communication with all of those on the spirit side of life.

You will explore the different categories of spirit guidance, and you will hear from the mediums themselves about their first contacts with the spirit world, as well as the various phenomena they have encountered.

- Noted mediums residing within a Spiritualist community share their innermost experiences, opinions, and advice regarding spirit communication
- Includes instructions for table tipping, automatic writing, and meditating to make contact with spirits
- For anyone interested in developing and understanding spiritual gifts

1-56718-530-4, 5⅜ x 8, 240 pp. glossary   **$9.95**

TO ORDER, CALL 1-877-NEW-WRLD
Prices subject to change without notice

TRUE HAUNTINGS
Spirits with a Purpose
Hazel M. Denning, Ph.D.

Do spirits feel and think? Does death automatically promote them to a paradise—or as some believe, a hell? Real-life ghostbuster Dr. Hazel M. Denning reveals the answers through case histories of the friendly and hostile earthbound spirits she has encountered. Learn the reasons spirits remain entrapped in the vibrational force field of the earth: fear of going to the other side, desire to protect surviving loved ones, and revenge. Dr. Denning also shares fascinating case histories involving spirit possession, psychic attack, mediumship, and spirit guides. Find out why spirits haunt us in *True Hauntings*, the only book of its kind written from the perspective of the spirits themselves.

1-56718-218-6, 240 pp., 6 x 9   **$12.95**

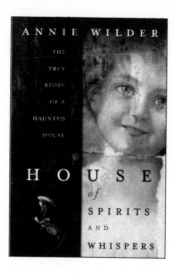

HOUSE OF SPIRITS & WHISPERS
The True Story of a Haunted House
Annie Wilder

When Annie Wilder and her two teenagers moved into an old Victorian house, she knew it would have some unusual features. A bedroom door that was too short and too narrow. An old-fashioned pull-handle toilet. A small cellar made of dirt with a latch on the inside of the door so that a person could lock himself in the basement.

From the time Annie moved in, the house spoke to her. First, the voice of her imagination told of secrets in its twisting halls. Then her dreams spoke to her. And finally, the murmurs of a ghost woke her from sleep. *House of Spirits and Whispers* is the true tale of how shadows from beyond awakened under Annie's roof.

Terrifying and thrilling, yet spiritually uplifting, it is an undefinable true story of a haunted house—one where fear is ultimately replaced with interest and care.

0-7387-0777-5, 158 pp. $12.95

MONSTERS

An Investigator's Guide to Magical Beings

Michael Greer

Shedding new light on those bone-chilling bumps in the night . . .

Most of us don't believe that entities such as vampires, shapeshifters, and faeries really exist. Even those who study UFOs or psychic powers dismiss them as unreal.

The problem is, people still keep running into them.

What do you do when the world you think you inhabit tears open, and something terrifying comes through the gap? Join ceremonial magician John Michael Greer as he takes you on a harrowing journey into the reality of the impossible. In *Monsters* he examines the most common types of beings still encountered in the modern world, surveying what is known about them and how you can deal with their antics.

0-7387-0050-9, 320 pp., 7½ x 9⅛, illus.   **$19.95**